Patterns for Successful IT Project Management

The Path to a Predictable Process

By K. J. Daniel

K. J. Daniel
1014 Gracewood Dr.
Libertyville, IL 60048

RUP ® and Rational Unified Process ® are trademarks of IBM

MSF ® is a trademark of Microsoft

ISBN 978-1-4303-2924-4

Sincere thanks goes to the hundreds of people who have worked with me throughout my career. This book is a result of what they taught me.

Words cannot express the appreciation for the support through the thick and thin times that was provided by my wife of 30 years.

Preface

Most of the books on software project management are very general. Many details are left to be filled in by the creativity of the reader. Without experience, filling in the blanks adds risk to the project. This book takes the reader an additional step and recommends patterns and processes based on experience. This is done in the spirit of identifying the minimum amount of ceremony needed to maximize the probability that the project will be a success.

This text is limited to a particular type of software development, data driven systems where a user modifies data in a database. There are many different classes of software. Each can benefit from a specialized management approach. This is different from most books on software project management that do not recognize that the application of software management could be different depending upon the type of software being constructed.

It is well recognized that the software industry has a poor record of being able to plan and execute a project that meets the triple constraint. One typical cause suggested is that requirements change. However, for most companies, over a period of several months, business processes do not change significantly. In fact changing a process in a particular business domain is very difficult. If the business processes do not change, why do requirements? Other studies suggest that too many requirements are typically gathered resulting in many software features that are not used. These facts point to a significant problem with the standard process for gathering requirements. Non-standard methods are described in this book, which provide more accurate requirements.

Industry trends are now moving toward Agile or XP that have no planning or a weak "plan as you go" methodology. The justification is that software deliverables are too unstable to be planned. The process is more like a football game than the orderly progression toward a goal. In some cases software projects are best managed with a reactive planning process. In the software domain that was chosen for this book, things are more stable. Data is inserted, displayed and updated in a database. Projects are very similar. They are not completely new designs. They are more like building row-houses that have slight variation. While many software projects cannot be easily executed using a measured and planned approach, projects in this domain can be performed using a controlled predictable process.

In my experience, I have found the techniques presented in this book, work exceptionally well. It is my hope that through the experience of others these techniques will be refined so that business can reliably predict the cost of IT development projects.

There are four major themes to this book: (1) get the requirements right using special patterns (2) use patterns to obtain a detailed and correct task list (3) automate the development as much as possible by configuring templates instead of writing code (4) use special patters to get good estimates.

This book is not meant to be a primer on software project management. There are many excellent texts on this topic like McConnel [1996], Kroll [2003], PMBOK [PMI, 2004] and Larman [2004]. Rather, this book assumes the reader has some software project experience and will benefit from recommendations that apply to the various stages of software development life cycle.

About the Author

Dr. Daniel has over 20 years of experience managing software development projects. He is currently a senior project manager for an international consulting company. The companies where he has applied his talents include: GE, US Bank, Monster.com, Dun and Bradstreet, Northwestern Mutual, Firestone and a variety of small companies.

Dr. Daniel holds a project management certification (PMP) and several technical certifications: Oracle DBA, Java Developer, VB.Net and C# Web Development. He also holds a software patent.

The author can be contacted at kenndaniel@yahoo.com

Table of Contents

Chapter 1 Introduction

Management vs. Leadership

In my mind there is a big difference between leading a project and managing a project. "Managing" is like an old milkman using a horse and wagon on his way home. The horse knows the way. The man only needs to hold on to the reins. By contrast, "leading" brings to mind a chariot race with the driver firmly in control of the horses as they complete the race.

A project leader is someone who has the big picture, understands the problem domain and also the technology. Project leaders know enough to evaluate tradeoffs when proposed by developers and can communicate well with the system stakeholders. They guide the team along the path and the team looks to them as a technical peer that they can rely on to provide the right direction. Project leaders are in control because they know what they are doing and have the respect of the team.

The analogy with a chariot race can be taken too far. Hopefully, the developers don't feel like overstressed horses at the end of a project. Successful projects have proper schedules. Team members understand where they are at all times and what is expected of them. The leader knows where the project is at all times and can keep clients informed. There is no unexpected crunch – death march – 16-hour day in the last phase.

Here's another analogy. Project management is like painting a picture. The paint and brush are the resources that you have and the final painting is the goal of your project. You apply the resources to the proper areas in order to produce something that the critics (stakeholders) accept and like. There are some rewarding creative aspects to project management. This is not only in applying resources, but also in dealing with issues and problems that arise.

The goal of this book is to provide important patterns for a leader of web development projects. In order to lead a project using these patterns, you will need to combine basic project management skills with basic technical knowledge and some creativity. The technology is closely tied to success. The leader needs to understand the effect of architecture on planning and scheduling.

Many project management patterns will be presented in the following chapters. They focus on the major obstacles to success and provide improved methods for overcoming them. The primary patterns address the following areas: (1) getting the requirements right (2) obtaining a detailed and correct task list (3) automating the development as much as possible by configuring templates instead of writing code (4) obtaining correct estimating.

The Perfect Project

It is easy to define what is not a perfect project. As an industry we are very good in regularly creating examples. Unfortunately, cost overruns and systems that do not come close to meeting user expectations are regular occurrences. Many times key requirements are missed and sometimes large amounts of additional functionality is added that is never utilized.

One part of the definition of a perfect project is that it provides the maximum amount of benefit for the least cost. No extraneous documentation is created, no rework is required to correct flawed requirements, and all functionality that has been coded is used by the business. The business needs that were the goal of the project are fulfilled.

The key to providing the maximum benefit for the least cost is to only create what is necessary for success. This requires that there be no wasted effort and no unnecessary ceremony.

This breaks down to several main tasks:

- Efficiently getting requirements correct so the delivered software satisfies the business need and the customer is satisfied with the system

- No functions are developed that will not be used

- The minimum amount of documentation is created

- The developers and testers have clear unambiguous instructions and goals

- A development process is used that is efficient and minimizes rework

- The team is kept as productive as possible.

As a whole, our industry is very poor at these tasks. The following chapters will focus on these topics.

There is another part to the definition of a perfect project. At the outset of a project, a business expects to get a particular amount of benefit from investing a particular amount of money. It is tempting to define a perfect project as one that meets these expectations. However, that is the ideal project not the perfect project. With the uncertainties that are inherent in the software development process this cannot be guaranteed. Upper management needs to realize investing in custom software development is no different than any other investment. All investment has risk. Software is no different.

The Predictable Project

Being able to predict the cost of providing the claimed benefits is a key problem for software development [Humphrey 1990]. The corporate annual planning cycle goes something like this. Management says,

> *"We need a new skyscraper building in Chicago. How much will it cost and what will the revenue be? Give me an estimate in two weeks. We will then make a final decision."*

This is clearly an example of poor management. Who would make a decision on such a large investment after only two weeks of analysis? Yet, this is what software development managers are regularly asked to do.

The impossible task of immediate estimates must be substituted with a process similar to other industries. Initial approval is given for an architect to draw up plans based upon preliminary estimates, and then make final decisions of the investment using estimates based on complete requirements. The predictable project works within these goals to create accurate plans and estimates with as little fanfare and ceremony as possible. The predictable project may not have accurate estimates initially, but it strives to provide accurate estimates as early as possible.

Many of the current project processes that are in vogue today fall short in this regard. They disregard any type of long range planning and justify this by saying that the business environment changes too rapidly to make accurate predictions of cost. However, the majority of business processes do not change rapidly. If you have ever attempted to become a change agent in a large corporation you will understand this. Rapid, massive change is uncommon. What is more common is the inability of the IT department to fully understand the business process and accurately communicate with the business. What is also common is the inability of the business to explain their processes.

For years, the "use case" has been the recommended method for clarifying the communications between business and development. Despite our poor track record of capturing requirements and providing extraneous functionality, this continues to be the standard for projects. Maybe it is time to reconsider the standard recommendation.

Data Driven Projects

It is the author's experience that one category of software represents a significant amount of IT development and maintenance effort. This category employs a user interface to create, read, update and delete records in a database. Most commonly they access only the data in only one database but could access several. Excluded from discussion are web sites that display unstructured data (text). These are best handled using content management systems.

The content of this book is concerned **only** with structured data driven software, which is common in the IT industry. Since the scope is limited to this type of development, a specific pattern for project management can be used. Every project of this type is not unique. It is more like building houses in a new development. The builder provides a few model homes that can be customized in various ways. The project is not a one-off construction of a unique architectural design.

This book is different than most books that approach this topic because it does not attempt to address a general software development approach that is broadly applicable to all segments of the software industry. It takes only a segment and looks at what can be done to make it into a predictable process.

The subject of this book will be further limited to IT web sites. People have been doing IT web development for years. Nothing is radically new and many management patterns have evolved that can be used to minimize both cost and risk. The extent to which a project fits these patterns, determines how predicable the project can be. In many cases web site implementation can be reduced to a repeatable, measurable, predicable process. The extension of the techniques to other types of data-driven sites is left for future studies and books.

Meeting the Triple Constraint

The following chapters will follow basic project management procedures using a controlled, iterative approach. What this means is that each iteration is performed professionally with good planning, tracking and delivery expectations with regard to function, schedule, and budget. Functionality, schedule, and cost are a project's triple constraint.

All projects, regardless of whether it is building a bridge or developing software, has the triple constraint as its goal. The constraints are closely tied. For example, decreasing the number of functions that are provided will reduce costs. The career of a typical IT project manager depends upon completing projects that meet or come close to meeting the triple constraint.

In this book we will not discuss ad hoc development iterations that do not commit to meeting the functionality constraint. This type of development process may have its place where there are large technical uncertainties or requirements cannot be gathered. In this type of project, the return for the investment of scarce development resources cannot be projected. This is not reality. In today's IT environment, projects compete for limited resources based upon the return on investment. After the money has been spent, the return must be there.

It is not being claimed that data driven web projects can be completely planned. What is being said is the risk and uncertainties can be minimized to a point where making commitments to meeting the triple constraint can be made. The manager does not need to fall back on ad hoc iterations with fuzzy functionality goals. This type of project ends up performing rework to correct requirements errors. It also wastes development time waiting for business people to make decisions on requirements that were not initially documented.

The shortest path between two points is a straight line. The two points are the beginning of the project and the end of the project. Minimize the rework caused by mistaken requirements and you take a large step towards minimizing the overall project cost. It also eliminates a large amount of uncertainty in the estimation process.

You must be thinking that all this sounds too good to be true. You're right. Nothing can guarantee success, but there is a great deal that can be done to minimize uncertainty and increase the probability of success. This results in a well-defined path from the beginning to the end of the project.

What wisdom there is in this book comes primarily from the successful and unsuccessful projects that I've been involved with for the last 20 years. This is integrated with and augmented by the collected wisdom of many current project management trends.

Risk

At many places in this book we will discuss risk. Risk management has become a popular topic in the last decade. Risk implies decreasing the probability that something will go wrong and planning for it if it does. Alternatively it can be looked at in an additional non-conventional way. Risk management is the performance of actions to increase the probability of success. Leading a project requires the manager to be ahead of the game and do tasks in a way that increases the probability of success. This is in addition to identifying and planning for the things that could go wrong.

Chapter 2 Development Process Overview

Iterative Development In an IT Environment

McConnel [1996] discusses many techniques for organizing a project. One of the major differences among these is how iterations are integrated into the process. Since the publishing of this classic text, other methodologies have come into vogue such as XP [Beck, 2001] and Agile [Larman 2004]. A full comparison of these processes is outside the scope of this book, but a quick overview of where following sections of this book lie is needed to give the reader some perspective.

If you look at all of the processes, they vary by the amount they integrate iteration into the process. The technique with the least amount of iteration is the waterfall process. At the other end of the spectrum is "code and ship" which is the ultimate iterative process. "Code and ship" until it is correct. Neither of these, according to McConnel and other books have a high probability of success. Between these two extremes is a virtual continuum of processes that integrate various amounts of iterations. Depending on many factors, each of these can lead to a successful project.

In books on software project management, there appears to be two extremes of iterative development. At the low structure end of iterative development is a plan-as-you-go type of iteration, which is represented by the XP process [Beck 2001]. This type of process relies on very short iterations on the order of weeks and there is no planning past the short iteration. It does not attempt to predict the functionality of the overall project. The project goal and definition of success changes as the project evolves. We will call this **pure iterative**.

The high end of structured iterative development splits large projects up into small ones of 3 – 6 months in duration. This is consistent with recommendations of Glib [Glib 1988] who was one of the founders of iterative development. Development of large systems should be split into phases. These are planned iterations with a production delivery at the end of each phase. Within each phase the project may be broken down into iterations that are not released but are production quality. We will call this first type of iterative development **planned iterative** development. The functionality in each of the iterations is planned.

Resource Availability -

Existing Business Processes - Many web systems are internal with well-defined user groups. The functionality is not driven by the whim of someone in marketing or the latest great idea about what the customer wants, but by a reasonably well-defined business processes like some special aspect of billing that needs to be automated. Over a three-to-six month period, processes of this type do not change rapidly unless something catastrophic happens, like a merger. With this exception, there is no excuse to not know what the business requirements are.

The big advantage of the pure iterative approach is that there is no commitment to meeting the triple constraint. At the beginning of the project it is stated that we will change the amount of functionality to make sure that we spend all of the allotted money in the scheduled period of time. This is a very attractive to project managers because you can be sure that the project will be on time and on budget and what ever is delivered with regard to functionality is OK. The structure assures success. If you can get your management to agree to this, it is the best way to manage a project. However, this type of planning does not fit well into the multiple project environments. It especially has difficulty in the fixed-cost consulting environment or with offshore distributed development teams. Moreover, it is not popular with upper management that would strongly prefer a predictable process [McConnell, 2006].

There are always more projects for an IT department to work on than there are resources. Before the project begins, there must be some estimate of the costs and benefits of the project. The planning process requires sensitivity to estimates and resource availability that spans simultaneous projects.

The pure iterative approach has been developed in response to the problem of rapidly changing requirements. Contrary to what is written in many books, the processes are relatively stable in business over a time span of a few months. In fact, in most businesses change of processes is resisted and difficult to implement. In many cases the problem is not that the requirements changed. The problem is that business requirements were not captured properly.

There are patterns that can be used to make sure the requirements are correct and to minimize the risks in estimates. These patterns use paper prototypes and storyboards of the system to extract user requirements.

Planned, iterative development fits well into an IT environment. What is being proposed here is that iterations be used in the requirements gathering phase. This phase consists primarily of quickly creating non-operating paper prototypes of the system. Following requirements gathering, the heavy lifting development can be performed using a planned iterative delivery approach without much rework. It has been well established that rework of code to correct requirements errors can be very expensive compared to making corrections earlier in the project. Using iterations to perfect requirements and prototypes to validate requirements are far less expensive.

The following is an example of the iterations that were used in an ecommerce application:

1. Paper prototype showing all desired functionality

2. Look and feel prototype(s) – to obtain agreement on the visual style. This consisted of two web pages showing colors and navigation menus.

3. HTML & graphics for all pages– Final look and feel

4. Catalog store functionality – search, product display

5. Checkout functionality -- basic registration and basic checkout

6. Data conversion and backend integration

7. Implementation of remaining UI functionality

Overall Process

PMO/Contracted Development Approach

This organization method breaks the project down into two distinct phases. The first phase obtains agreement on the requirements and the second phase concentrates on phased development and delivery (Figure 2.1). The first three steps in the example of the previous section fall into the iterative requirements phase. Within each of these steps were iterations. The last four steps fall into the iterative delivery category.

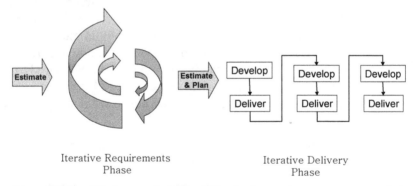

Iterative Requirements Phase

Iterative Delivery Phase

Figure 2.1 Simplified conceptual view of the development process recommended for web projects.

Each phase of the recommended phases is estimated separately. This fits many corporate project portfolio management (PPM) environments where approval is given to perform the detailed requirements and then final approval is given to proceed with the completion of development. This minimizes corporate risk because decisions are based on more accurate estimates than what can be provided by only an initial estimate.

This two-phase approach provides maximum control and management visibility of the resources that are being invested in software. It also works well with offshore development staff. The paper prototypes and associated descriptions leave little to be misunderstood.

Market Driven Approach

The previous process was optimized to provide accurate estimates before a significant amount of resources were spent. This will increase the overall duration (not cost) of a project because reasonably complete requirements are created before development begins. However, if time-to-market is the most important criterion, a different approach may be taken.

Development may begin as soon as the requirements are gathered and approved for a subset of the system. The only risk is that the project may be cancelled based upon the first phase estimates and development work will be scrapped. Upper management should be informed of this risk and they should make the decision for proceeding with development before the first phase is complete.

In this case the process reduces to be very similar to a normal iterative approach. However, if one thinks about this methodology, it is really a phased development approach, not iterative. Iterative implies a perfecting process. Each iteration needs to be corrected and embellished with the new requirements that are discovered. Sections of carefully tested code may need to be thrown away. On the other hand, with paper prototype iteration, only parts of inexpensive paper prototypes need to been thrown away. Development can proceed without rework for requirements errors.

Large Projects

The proposed process is applicable for small projects, however, the risk with large projects increases significantly. Breaking the project down into parts that can be handled by small teams, is the key. This is similar to the organization of the Roman army that was very successful at reaching large goals.

> *Centuries (commanded by centurions) were nominally 80 soldiers each (not 100, as is popularly believed), but in practice might be as few as 60..... Each century had its standard and was made up of ten units called* contubernia. *In a contubernium, there would be eight soldiers who shared a tent, millstone, a mule and cooking pot. Each contubernia was led by an officer called a Decurion*
>
> [Wikipedia http://en.wikipedia.org/wiki/Roman_legion]

The optimum team size appears to be 10 or less. A reasonable time duration is 3-9 months. Projects requiring more than this need to be broken down into subprojects. Of course with large teams it is well known that there are inefficiencies that must be accounted for due to the number of communications channels among the team members. For planning purposes a lower bound for the project resources requirements can be obtained by not accounting for these interactions.

Project Roles

Subject Matter Experts --The Agile development process, which is a pure iterative development process growing in popularity, claims that there is no need for the business analyst to work with the business to document their needs. It recommends that business experts (sometimes called subject matter experts or SME) work directly with developers. In many cases this causes delays and miscommunication. One or two SMEs cannot effectively communicate with a team of 10 developers and still do their normal job. Moreover, the best developers are not chosen for their business knowledge or their ability to communicate. Some can do an excellent job at this and others are not as skilled. This introduces project risk.

SMEs are typically the experts in the particular area of the business that will use the delivered software. Because they are the business experts they are in high demand by the business and not always available to answer questions and provide reviews when needed. This adds schedule and cost risk to the project. It is better to have one business analyst working with the erratic schedules of SMEs than having a team of developers sitting around waiting until the SMEs have time.

The use of a business analyst to quickly document the requirements in a form that is readily understandable by both the business, the testing team and the development team is key to minimizing this risk. The business analyst is the leader in the first phase, documenting processes and creating paper prototypes for review by business.

> *Pattern: Requirements are negotiated not just gathered.*

The business analyst must provide one more important function. They must challenge the business on frivolous requests. They should not just take dictation. Custom software is expensive. Developing unused and unnecessary functionality is a waste of company resources and lengthens schedules. Each function that is documented for development needs an estimate of its importance and frequency of use. The business analyst needs the authority to be able to push back (using tact and diplomacy).

Every project requires different skills. On some project teams one person could play many roles. In large organizations or large projects, different people in different departments typically fill the roles. On smaller projects, the project manager performs many of these roles and many of the other roles are combined.

At a minimum, for a web project you need the following roles:

Project Manager – Responsible for issue tracking/resolution, staffing, planning, measuring progress, reporting status and various other tasks.

Business Analyst – Responsible for communicating the requirements of the desired system from the business stakeholders to the development team.

System Analyst – Fleshes out high-level requirements into specifications that have a sufficient level of detail that allows accurate estimation and coding.

Data Analyst – Responsible for the enterprise data model. They know where data is stored and are responsible for the design of a new, or extension of existing enterprise databases. The role of the data analyst in the modern organization must be expanded to not only keep track of the enterprise data model, but also the enterprise data services.

Architect – Responsible for the use of the enterprise software architecture. A later section of this book will be devoted to explaining the enterprise software architecture. At this point, the role certifies that the product of this project bares some resemblance architecturally to other systems currently in use.

Web Designer – Capable of creating beautiful static html pages.

Developer – a Java or .Net capable developer that breathes life into the static web pages.

Tester – responsible for designing tests that qualify the system based upon system requirements

Support Developer – a developer that is responsible for making modifications to the system after delivery.

Management Stakeholder – Business-side project champion. Does not use the system, but supports the development and aids in obtaining funding.

User Stakeholders (Users) – People who will be affected by the system when complete. You should have access to a representative sample of users to provide requirements, answer questions and participate in acceptance testing.

Operations Support Personnel -- There will also be a wide variety of other people that support the hardware and network environment. These special roles are critical for success.

It is the job of the project manager to orchestrate the work of the people in these roles to attain the objectives of the project (artist). It requires managing upward in the organization, downward to subordinates and across to other departments. Much of this work is managing through influence (across) laterally in an organization. Unfortunately, this is a skill that is not easily taught. It requires creativity, good judgment, and an understanding of people and sometimes politics. I wish I could teach this. The demand would be great and I would be one of the few teachers that are in high demand.

Minimum Ceremony

The perfect project produces the minimum amount of documentation necessary to assure success and to satisfy user requirements. Documentation is expensive to produce and maintain. Industry literature abounds with different types of documentation that is recommended. This fact is highlighted in IBM documentation as illustrated by the following quotes from an article titled *The Ten Essential Parts Of RUP:*

Often, as I help project teams sort through the many elements in RUP (at last count, I found 4 phases, 9 core workflows, 31 workers, 103 artifacts, 136 activities, plus more guidelines, checklists and tool mentors than I would care to count!), I hear questions such as: "How do I sort through all of these items and determine which I need for my project?" "Do I need this one?" "Isn't RUP only for big projects?"" ...

"Remember, each project team should come up with their own list. My list of ten essentials is only meant as a starting point for further discussion."
[Probasco 2000]

The Unified Process (UP) is one of the most popular software project management methodologies in use today. One of UP's strengths is its flexibility. It is a collection of industry standards. This work will pick parts of UP appropriate for IT web development projects and combine it with principles of good project management from the Project Management Book of Knowledge (PMBOK) [PMI 2004], which is published by the Project Management Institute.

Chapter 3 Inception Project Charter

Whimsical list of the 6 stages of a project:

1. Wild enthusiasm

2. Disillusionment

3. Total confusion

4. Search for the guilty

5. Punishment of the innocent

6. Promotion of the non-participants

[Anonymous]

Starting a project with enthusiasm is a good thing. It gets the project off to a good start. The other items I hope you only experience from a distance.

Inception Phase Goals

The focus of the inception phase is to gain initial approval for the first phase of the project and to gather requirements to support the later project tasks.

Project Initial Approval

The first task in the inception phase is to obtain business approval for the project. This is consistent with the project management principles mentioned in the PMBOK. Typically this is accomplished by creating a short document (1-5 pages) that state three things (1) the major business benefits that the project plans to provide, (2) the organization(s) that will be affected and (3) how they will be affected. This document is sometimes called the project charter.

Business management must approve the charter. This provides the go ahead to start the detailed requirements gathering and project planning effort.

Another large cause for system failure is the lack of upper management support. The document approvers are the people who can provide or can obtain the upper management support. They are also the people who can stop the project if later cost estimates indicate a lower than expected ROI. The corporate culture should allow for this situation without repercussions.

To create the charter, a significant but not overwhelming amount of information needs to be assembled. The exact content needed for approval is organization dependent. Critical to approval is the business benefits and business case. Another name for business benefits are business-level requirements. These are what the system is expected to provide the business. A major cause for project failure is not having a clear business case. By approving the charter, management is agreeing that the business case is sound. This also provides the initial go ahead for the first phases of the project.

Other information is also typically needed. Almost always a project must compete for funding based upon the magnitude of the return on the investment (ROI). In order to evaluate this the value of the benefits and the cost of the project are needed. Many times, high-level functionality is identified and limitations are placed on the project scope. Users are identified that will be affected by the system. An initial description of the system functions is documented. Risk analysis is also provided to identify the factors that have a high probability of preventing the attainment of the business benefits. An initial project plan is needed to identify when the business benefits would be realized. The timing of the benefit could affect the evaluation of the benefits.

Unfortunately, at this point in the project there are large uncertainties. A cost estimate is needed to calculate the ROI. Project managers shudder at trying to estimate the cost of a project with so little information. There is no easy answer. Projects typically turn out to be much larger than the original estimate. Fearful project managers sometimes purposefully overestimate by large amounts to protect themselves. However, this could prevent valuable systems from being developed due to exaggerated estimates. Prudent IT organizations will realize the uncertainty in these numbers and plan for this risk. There is nothing the project manager can do at this time to make the estimate more certain. However, from an IT organization point of view, much can be done to make estimates consistent among the projects being proposed for funding. This point will be discussed in a later chapter on the role of the project management office (PMO).

As a project progresses, understanding of the work increases. Figure 3.1 shows a classic chart of estimating uncertainty. The trends of this graph are clear. As a project gets closer to the finish there are fewer uncertainties and cost estimates become more accurate. The actual values on the graph should not be taken seriously. The study is relatively old and is not representative of all software types. What this graph shows is that initial estimates are not going to be accurate. This makes the planning process for an enterprise difficult. Multiple projects must be compared based upon highly inaccurate estimates. Project manages are temped to over estimate because they will be responsible for delivering at the estimated cost.

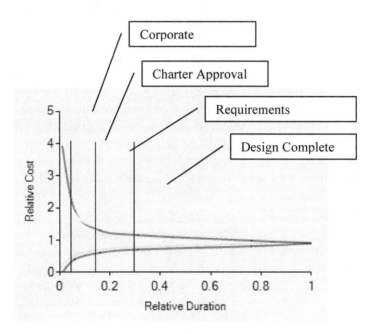

Figure 3.1 The Cone of Uncertainty Adapted from "Cost Models for Future Lifecycle Processes: COCOMO 2.0" Boehm, et. al., [1995] (iv). The x-axis tick marks correspond roughly to the charter approval (.05), requirements complete (.15), and project plan complete (.3).

In reality, the project manager has little control over the outcome of a project if the estimates are wrong. Management should realize the uncertainty in software estimates and other information in the charter. They should request and expect updates that are more accurate as the project becomes better defined.

The Project Management Office should be responsible for the quality assurance with regard to the project management process that is employed on a project. The project manager should be evaluated based upon adherence to the process and other factors, not the final cost of the project based upon the information available at the time of the charter. Adherence to the process should ensure that the enterprise gets software at the lowest possible cost.

Enterprise Planning Pattern

It is becoming more common to plan software investment using a two-step process. First an estimate is provided for the completion of the requirements gathering/design phases. The result of this first phase then provides a basis for planning the remainder of the project. The estimate for the following development phase is created based upon detailed requirements instead of high-level wishes.

Even using the previous technique, correct project schedules are difficult in many cases because of personnel issues such as the productivity of developers and variations in code quality from developers. Tasks of a project will not be estimated exactly. Some will be higher and some lower than the estimates. Contingency is also necessary to account for uncertainties. Note that the process is not totally unpredictable. We are not trying to develop a Gant chart for a football game. Figure 3.2 shows the accuracy of estimates for a real project made after requirements were defined. It shows a comparison between the estimated and actual task applied time. A high degree of predictability is indicated.

In the software domain that was chosen for this book, data is inserted, displayed and updated in a database. Projects of this type are very similar. They are not completely new designs. They are more like building row houses that have slight variation. While many software projects cannot be easily executed using a measured and planned approach, projects in this domain can be successfully completed using a well-controlled process.

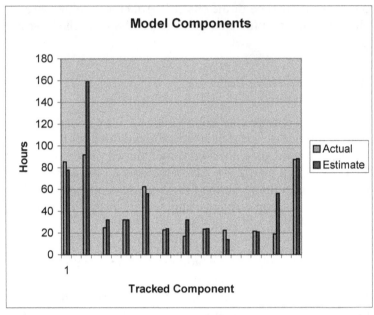

Fig ure 3.2 Actual and estimated time for the model component development tasks of a real project.

Schedules can be made that are reasonably close to what is needed to deliver the needed software. A later chapter of this book is dedicated to presenting estimating patterns that have been found successful on real projects.

Business Analysis

For this discussion, business analysis begins after the business case has been established and ends when all stakeholders and the business analyst have a mutual understanding of the operation of the final system. This is basically the requirement gathering/negotiating phase.

Chapter 4 Project Scope

Requirements should be based upon what the user will see in the end result and **easy for the user to understand and validate.**

One key indicator of proper requirements is that the users have a clear understanding of what will be delivered and they have agreed that it is what they need. Coming to this understanding is not easy. Consequently, this is the major topic covered in the next sections. Patterns for iterative requirements gathering using a paper prototype technique are presented. They provide quick inexpensive iterations that help the clients and the IT department understands the problem and agrees to the solution.

> *"Lack of user input, incomplete requirements, and changing requirements are the major reasons why information technology projects do not deliver all of their planned functionality on schedule and within budget."[Standish 1994]*

Not Enough or Too Many Requirements

Studies have shown that a major cause of system failure is the inability to accurately capture system requirements. On the other hand, there are studies that have also documented problems with gathering requirements that result in software features that never get used. So as an industry, we are simultaneously guilty of both gathering too many and not enough requirements. This contradiction has two valid conclusions. The first is that good requirements gathering cannot be done. This has led to new development management approaches such as XP and Agile. The other conclusion is that the way we gather requirements may be flawed. Perhaps the dogma of using use cases for everything is not correct.

Requirements Gathering Process

Let's look at the main purpose of requirements.

1. Document the new process that the system will support.

2. Provide an easily understandable preview of the system to the users so they can critically review and critique it before development begins.

3. Provide enough information so that development can begin design and testers develop a test plan.

The shortest distance between two points is a straight line. In project management this means that from the beginning to the end of the project there are no changes or errors that cause rework. Everything is gotten right the first time. Minimum cost is closely related to minimum rework. Rework can be caused by changing requirements, errors in understanding the requirements (requirements error), or programming defects. The first of these is out of the control of the project manager and are handled with approved change requests that modify the budget. However we are on the hook for the last two. These can be minimized by using special techniques.

Anti-patterns for Gathering Requirements

At this point let's take a look at some of the common process defects that can affect the success of the project.

Type 1 Inadequate Review / Misunderstanding

Requirements errors are very common. In the real world, I have seen project where, what development delivers genuinely surprises the users. They signed off on the requirements without fully understanding them.

Many excellent books describe the requirements gathering process. They provide a multitude of techniques, but few recommendations. Most people in the computer industry believe that developing a set of use cases is the best method of documenting requirements. Although my experience is not as comprehensive as many, I have seen and have heard of many failed projects that have relied on use cases to document and communicate requirements. In most instances the miss application of use cases was a significant contributing factor.

The business analysis function serves as a translator between the business and the development team. Many times the analyst comes from a programming background and thinks in a programming mindset. They attempt to extract requirements from members of the business community who have a different vocabulary and mindset. Because of the different vocabulary and mind set, when one person explains a concept a slightly different concept is understood by the listener. Because of communication problems like this, using only words to describe requirements should be considered high risk.

Hopefully the business analyst is chosen because they are bilingual and can speak equally well to business representatives and developers. However, what vocabulary should be used for requirements documents? If the business vocabulary is used, the users can review and approve the use cases, but can the use case now be fully understood by the development team?

Even if the use cases are in business vocabulary, there can be problems. The business people typically have many demands on their time. Use cases for a complex system are sometimes very dry reading. In order for them to contain enough information to develop an accurate software product, many details must be included. Reviewing them requires a significant amount of time to absorb properly and catch the mistakes. This takes smart, detailed-minded people that have a good deal of spare time. If the use cases are not carefully reviewed, problems occur when the user sees the result. The typical standoff occurs. The business stakeholder says, "This is not what I wanted." The project manager says, "But it's what the use case said." No one wins in this situation. Either the customer is remains unhappy/inefficient or significant rework is required.

A prudent project manager should not rely on business people carefully reading use cases. People in business typically have many immediate demands placed on them and do not have enough time to read long documents containing minutia. To circumvent this process in past positions, the author gathered people together and read through the requirements as a group. He will never do that again. People become easily board and when you lose their attention effective review is impossible.

Also consider what the risk would be in creating a document of "what should be done" and sending it half way around the world for implementation. Would you accept the risk inherent in assuming the ability of the developer to read and perfectly understand English written in the US?

In almost every industry, cost is a constant concern. A great deal of time is spent on how to make process more efficient and at the same time becomes more effective. In the case of requirements the state-of-the-art is use cases. Use cases have not evolved in 15 years despite our poor record of being able to capture requirements. We tediously write out use cases that take a great deal of time to write and are difficult and time consuming to read. This is interesting because one of the mantras of the well-known UP process is to *model visually*, yet the state of the art for requirements is to bury everything in mounds of text.

In the following sections, examples will be given of techniques to make requirements documents more clear so that:

- Developers can quickly grasp what is to be developed.

- Testers can efficiently develop test plans.

- Users can easily critically evaluate what is to be delivered before it is developed.

Achieving these two points will eliminate a major project risk. Subject matter experts (SME) are the business people who provide and review requirements. They are typically the most knowledgeable people in a particular area of business. Because of this they have many demands on their time. They may not have the time necessary to read tomes of boring stuff. Those that are good at reading long, boring documents and have the time, can critically evaluate a system described in use cases. But this implies risk in relying on the reading skill and availability of the SME. It doesn't matter how many signatures you have on the requirements document. You may have covered yourself, but the business looses out when requirements are flawed. Time and money is spent on costly rework.

Type 2 Not going far enough

The conventional wisdom stated in books is that requirements should focus on what should be done not how it is done. It should not be concerned with how these functions will be performed. On the surface this makes sense. However, in practice, without getting user agreement on how something is done, many missed requirements are not found until late in the project.

The process goes something like this:

A man goes to a tailor and asks for a suit to be made for him. The tailor takes the man's measurements and asks if he will wear the suit to church or to parties. The man says, "Parties." "Good," says the tailor. "I have your functional requirements I will go an design your suit. We are using iterative development here. Come back in six weeks and I will show you the pants."

The man comes back in 6 weeks and the tailor holds up the pants. "Oh, I wanted cuffs and I don't like bell bottoms. The tailor says, "No problem, just sign this change order and I will give you what you want. The pants that I produced are completely consistent with the functional requirements." The man looks at the cost of the change order and the balance in his checking account and then says, "Can you change the color?" "Yes, I will modify the change order to include that," says the tailor. The man looks at the new price and exclaims. "It looks like I can only afford the pants."

Type 3 Scope Creep

The scenario above has an alternate ending. In this story the tailor gets complete requirements, and shows the customer sketches of the final product. The tailor executes flawlessly and produces the suit on time and on budget. The customer comes and tries on the suit and it fits perfectly. However, now that the customer has tried on the suit he realizes that he would like to have an extra pocket on the inside. This is scope creep and is a real problem.

> *There are two industries in the United States that call their clients users. In both cases, when the user gets a little, they want more and more.*
> *Anonymous*

Type 4 User Gold Plating

Another form of scope creep can occur early in the requirements phase. The story goes something like this. The user of the system has been waiting for years to finally get on the priority list for a new system. She knows that IS has a large backlog and getting productivity enhancements for her team after the base system is completed may never happen. Consequently, every conceivable feature is requested for the system. Many of them will never be used. To get around this problem, users should be required to provide an importance grade to each feature, and they should not be allowed to use the same grade twice. In order to meet the needed ROI some of the less important functions may need to be dropped. Remember, at this point there is no approval to move forward with development.

Type 5 Theoretically Correct

Consider yourself lucky if designers and developers come up with a system that the uses like without paper prototypes. I have seen systems fail because users needed to create a telephone number record using a separate window before creating a new sales contact using that number. This is the result of a perfectly normalized database without user considerations.

Type 6 The Actual User

Until this point the discussion has been primarily about Intranet projects where the user is within the company. With Internet web projects the product manager substitutes for the user. Beware of product managers. Strongly suggest that actual users be in the requirements loop and provide their opinion. There has been at least one project manager looking for a job after his former company spent millions of dollars completing and getting ready to rollout a complex system only to find the customers refused to use it.

Type 7 Missed anomalies

Is the system expected to work properly when a zip code spans the state line? The business analyst should ask many questions about anomalies. Users typically are familiar with odd situations that are difficult to handle or are special cases. These must be included in the requirements not discovered in user acceptance testing or after the system is moved to production.

The Requirements Pattern

The solution is collaboration between the users and the analyst to find out the most efficient way the system functions should be done from a users perspective. Figure 4.1 shows the path to obtaining this definition.

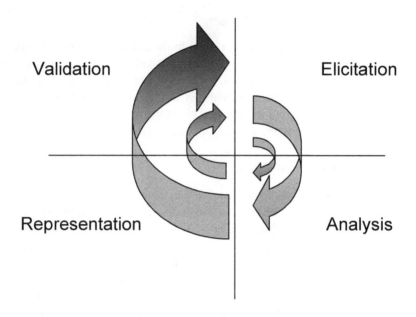

Figure 4.1 The iterative requirements gathering process.

Elicitation – Talking with users and stakeholders to gain an understanding of the business problems and how they should be solved.

Analysis – Assimilating various inputs into a proposed solution and comparing inputs with the scope of the project. Identifying gold plating user requests.

Representation – Expressing the proposed solution in an easily digestible format.

Validation – Making sure that the solution expressed in the documentation is understood by users and the stakeholders. Perfecting the requirements by obtaining meaningful reviews of the representation.

Figure 4.1 depicts a non-conventional iterative approach. The initial loops it starts with IT and the business documenting and agreeing on the business process that is to be automated. Once agreement is reached it continues iterating paper prototypes of the user interface that will be used to implement the process. In some cases working through the user interface design causes changes to the proposed business process. It has been my experience that sometimes the process is so well defined and understood that the process definition phase can be eliminated with no risk. In these cases the process starts with developing the prototype.

Prototype Iteration

> *Prototyping allows pre-development testing from many perspectives, especially usability, and helps create a better understanding of user interaction. It also leads to improved product specifications.(Microsoft, 2002b).*

In order to be efficient, iterations need to be as tight as possible. For example, an error in understanding the requirements should be corrected before coding is begun. Identifying a requirements error after coding is complete is expensive and a waist of resources. It would be much better to iterate in the requirement-gathering phase and validate the requirements before implementing the requirement in code.

In traditional OOA iterative processes, the first look that a user has of a system is an executable iteration. Much work goes into creating an executable iteration. HTML must be developed. Programmers must then breathe life into the static web pages. Much of this work will need to be redone based upon user comments. In order to eliminate this costly rework, the proposed process starts with simple paper prototypes that have an iteration cycle time of minutes not days. This short inexpensive iterative cycle is far less costly than OOA methods.

Use cases are only one tool in the bag of the business analyst. Instead, they need to use the tool that fits the problem being addressed. See the Table 4.1 below for a list of the minimum tool bag.

User/business element	Requirement capture type
Business Process	Use case or process diagram with swim lanes
Workflow	Use case or process diagram and state table
User interface	Paper prototype

Table 4.1 Recommend methods of requirements capture

Relying totally on use cases to document the requirements for a project might work adequately, but it is a high risk path. A lower risk approach to the gathering process is to use various techniques. The technique should be the one best suited to the requirement that is being defined.

The emphasis should be on the ability to communicate. What is being documented must be communicated efficiently to the uses, testers and the development team. Words should be the vehicle of documenting the minutia that is needed to explain details that are not fully described in the diagrams. Examples will be given in the next section.

Users and stakeholders have limited time and in many cases documents are not read in detail. Using a variety of more visual methods of capturing requirements can minimize the risk of inadequate review. This is done in the spirit of the "Model Visually" mantra of RUP. This not only increases the probability that what is delivered will satisfy the customer, but it is also more cost effective. Visual models are created and reviewed more quickly. "A picture is worth 1000 words," is true with requirements.

Process Diagram

Figure 4.2 shows a conventional process diagram. This type of diagram has been used for many years in process engineering. Horizontally there is a row for tasks done by the developer and a similar row for a tester. These are called swim lanes. Each rectangle represents a task. A diamond shape represents a conditional branch. Each of these are connected by arrows which signify the sequencing of the tasks. These diagrams can become complex as shown in the following examples. Regardless of the complexity, users can quickly understand the flow of the process and provide critical comments.

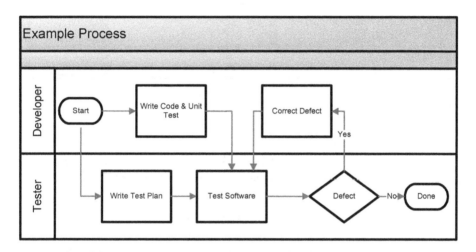

Figure 4.2 Example Process Diagram

Example 1 Process

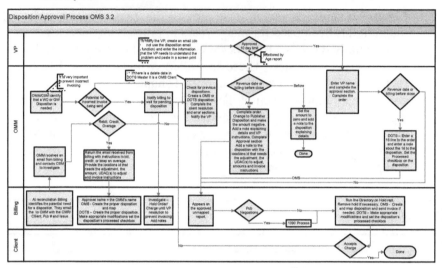

Figure 4.3 Real-world process diagram

Many times the first step an analyst must perform is to get the business to agree on what the business process is. Following this agreement, a user interface can be specified to support the process.

Figure 4.3 represents a real business process. Although you cannot read the text, you can easily understand how branches (diamond shapes) and processes (rectangles) are connected to document the overall process. This process flow diagram has swim lanes. Imagine how difficult this would be to understand if described in use cases. Imagine going into a meeting with representatives of different departments and leading a discussion about what the process should be. You hand out your best guess of how you think it should go. If your hand out is in use case format, people need to read and struggle with the words. If it's a diagram, discussion of important points starts quickly after a simple walk through.

Example 2 Workflow Process

Figure 4.4 and Table 4.2 show a variation of a process diagram without the optional swim lanes. The process tracks the processing of a billing dispute through various user roles. Instead of swim lanes the actor is indicated in the bottom of the action rectangle e.g. AE. Other than these minor differences both types of diagrams provide the same information. They are equivalent.

The arrows connecting the objects in the diagram are numbered. This provides a method to specify additional details about the interaction of the system with the process. Each step of the process is numbered. Each row of the table describes what the user and the system will do to complete the step. This is a rather simple example that illustrates an alternate method of process specification. All of the information in the table could have been placed within the boxes of the process diagram.

Note that there are two steps #3. They have the same initial status, but have different final end status based upon the user action performed. This represents a branch. Also note that there are two steps that have the same end status. This is because there they both have the same destination process step.

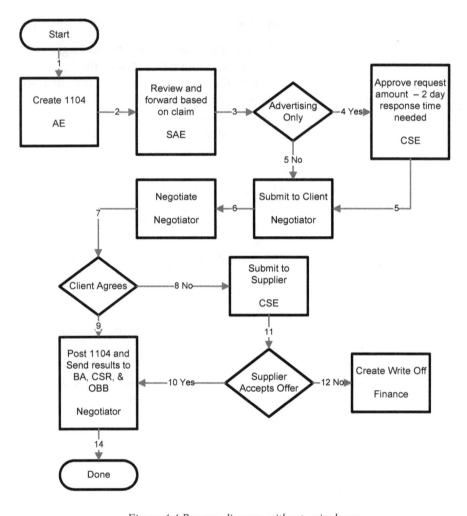

Figure 4.4 Process diagram without swim lanes

Using a step table is not as easy to understand as placing all of the information into the process rectangles. Consequently, it should be used sparingly. Its strength is that it methodically verifies that the paper prototype truly supports the process being automated. For large complex process, this can help minimize the errors.

Another advantage is that it helps bridge the gap between the process diagram and development. If the process is tracked as to how many disputes are in what status, the developer needs to know how to determine what the status of the dispute is. The table provides that information.

Step #	Initial Status	User Action	System Action	Final Status
1	Start	Data on tab A & Value Assigned on tab B		2. Ready for SAE Review
2.	Ready for SAE Review	CSE Reviewed checked on Tab b		3. SAE Reviewed
3	SAE Reviewed	Any box under Advertising Error is checked		4. Ready for CSE Approval
3	SAE Reviewed	No box under Advertising Error is checked		5 Ready to submit
4	Ready for CSE Approval	Authorized box on tab B checked		5 Ready to submit

Table 4.2 Partial state table showing the operations performed for each process step

Consequently in a workflow management application, where there could be hundreds of disputes in various stages of resolution, the status table is an aid more for communicating to the development team than it is to support user understanding.

The number of screens and database operations should be easily derived from the requirements. The following two examples show techniques for clearly defining to the users and developers the final system.

Example 3 User Interface

After the process/workflow diagrams are complete, quick non-working prototypes can be rapidly generated and provide the users a vision of what the product will do. What is being recommended are paper representations of the screens that will be in the system.

Paper screen can be taken to meetings and reviewed with users. This type of requirements validation is effective because the visual representation is more concrete and easier to understand than the words in the use cases. Concepts are communicated faster and mistakes are more easily identified. More importantly, iterations (additional reviews) can be rapidly performed with little cost. Moreover when the business stakeholders provide their approval, there is a better chance that no requirement errors will be discovered.

A paper prototype can be produced in minutes. Note, prototypes at this point do not need to be visually appealing or implemented in HTML. I have used MS Access, Excel, Paint and Visual Studio to mock up screens for a non-working prototype. The emphasis is on representing the functionality not visual design. The emphasis is also on minimizing coding rework. Having a web designer spend hours and hours making sure a prototype page looks perfect is unnecessary. A simple layout with all the envisioned fields and buttons is all that is needed.

The author has used paper prototypes and working prototypes on the same project. More meaningful comments were received with paper prototypes than with working prototypes. Although evidence is only anecdotal, it appears that users faced with a working prototype focus on how to use the prototype and not on how things should be done. They become mesmerized with clicking buttons. Users provide many more critical comments and recognize flaws easier when looking at a paper prototype.

In review meetings, paper prototypes are used to walk through how the business process will be accomplished with the new system. The prototypes easily feedback to the users the information they initially provided to the analyst. The discussions of these prototypes typically quickly identify problems and enhancements. Sometimes discussions and disagreements will be generated among multiple subject matter experts. The result will be a validation or correction of the requirements.

This example shows the specification of a user interface using a paper prototype. Figure 4.5 was created in 10 minutes using MS Access. A screen shot was taken and then pasted into the requirements document. The table (Table 4.3) and Business Rules and allowed user groups were then added. This process was repeated for all the pages in the system.

Figure 4.5 Paper prototype for one window of an investment application

Attribute	Default	Integrity Constraint
Old Security Number	blank	9 characters text
New Security	Unchecked	
(Old) Investment No	Output Only	
(Old) CUSIP	Output Only	
(Old) Exchange	Output Only	
(New) Investment No	Output Only	
(New) CUSIP	Output Only	
(New) Exchange	Output Only	

Table 4.3 Data initial condition and constraint table for paper prototype in Figure 4.5

Business Rules

This page will enable a user to update an investment key, with an existing investment vehicle key number. Following rules must be applied in implementing this functionality.

1) The user specifies an old and a new key then presses load (note that the update button is initially disabled).

2) The lower part of figure 5 is filled in with the appropriate information.

3) If the new key is already in the database or the old key is not in the database an error message will be given.

Allowed User Groups

View – All

Update – Sr. Auditors

Example 4 User Interface

This example is for a different application, but uses techniques similar to Example 3.

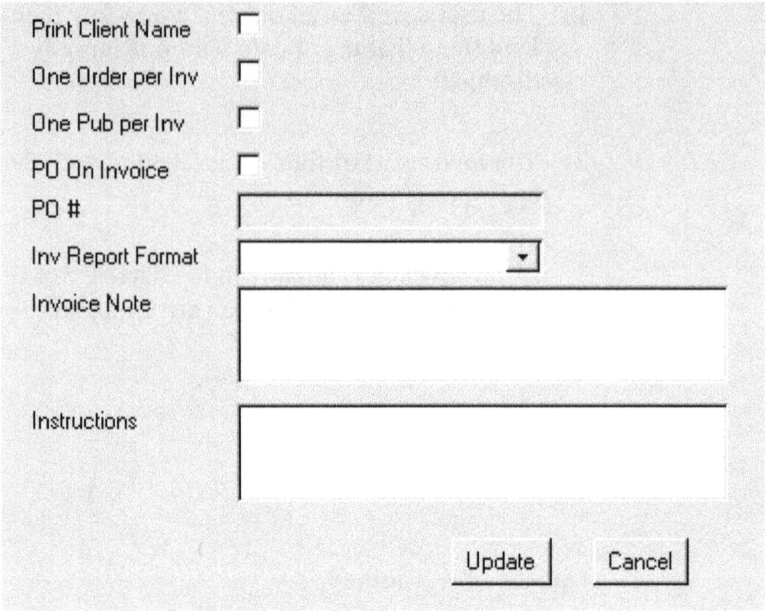

Print Client Name ☐

One Order per Inv ☐

One Pub per Inv ☐

PO On Invoice ☐

PO #

Inv Report Format

Invoice Note

Instructions

Update   Cancel

Figure 4.6 Paper prototype of the Invoice page.

Attribute	Default	Integrity Constraint
Print client name	Unchecked	
One order per invoice	Unchecked	
One pub per invoice	Unchecked	
Purchase Order on Invoice indicator	Unchecked	
Purchase Order #	Disabled unless the above item	Alphanumeric

		is checked.
Note on invoice – A note that will be placed on the invoice	Blank	Text
Printing instruction– Internal TMP instruction	Blank	Text
Inv report format	Blank	Dropdown of Formats

Table 4.4 Data initial condition and constraint table for paper prototype in Figure 4.6

Apply

An apply button will apply the entered changes.

Spell Check

Spell check should work for the note on invoice and printing instruction field.

Business Rules

The PO # should be disabled unless the PO on invoice is checked.

If PO on invoice is checked, PO # is required.

Allowed User Groups

View – All

Update – Sr. Order Auditors and Order Managers

User Navigation

The above examples do not include the menu structure for the site nor does it include any system level operations like a special print this page button. These need to be defined and reviewed with the users also using a paper prototype. These functions could have been included on Figure 4.5 and 4.6.

User Requirements Documentation Checkpoint

At the end of the requirements phase for each section of the system, the following should be defined for each page:

1. Data Requirements for each page

2. Data field types, sizes, validations rules and default values

3. Business rules that affect combinations of fields

4. Authorization groups for each page

5. Business rules for button actions

Chapter 5 Preparing to Estimate

An accurate estimate of a project's cost cannot be determined until a significant amount of work is done. Even after performing this work, without proper management and control, cost can still vary significantly from the estimate. However, the best management and control cannot make up for a poor estimate.

In order to complete an estimate, at a minimum you need:

- Definition of the architecture

- Definition of non-obvious functional requirements that integrate the user requirements to existing databases and systems

- The requirements need to be converted to development tasks. The development tasks represent the work breakdown structure for the project.

- Preliminary logical database design

- The developers need to understand the requirements and architecture and be capable of utilizing them to create the estimates for the tasks.

The tasks are clear and look formidable, but if kept pragmatic, the amount of effort required to complete the tasks can be manageable. They are also critical to the success of the project.

Functional Requirements

At this point in the project the business analyst has been deeply involved and has the requirements firmly in hand. Eventually this needs to be communicated to the web designers, developers and the data administrator. This requires that high-level requirements must be fleshed out to a sufficient level of detail that allows for estimation and coding. This has proven to be not nearly as difficult as it sounds. With the prototype as the guide, what needs to be documented becomes obvious and the documentation is straightforward. The format of the documentation should be chosen to facilitate rapid creation and unambiguous reading. The correct level of ceremony and verboseness must be chosen. Keep focused on the goals stated in the following paragraphs.

The two items that typically cause project schedules to go awry are:

- The overlooked task – some task found during development that was not accounted for on the original schedule.

- The exploding task -- estimated as a much smaller task, but when development begins it is recognized to be huge.

Many times these problems are caused by planning at a high lever without sufficient details to support the plan. The techniques described in the following sections have been used to minimize these risks. They are a type of mental prototype that forces a detailed mental walk through of the system. This identifies details that could cause estimation mistakes.

The project charter has defined the requirements from the business perspective. Chapter 4 discussed the collection of user requirements. What are remaining are the functional requirements. Functional requirements define the details of how the new system must integrate with the current environment. No system is an island. It must integrate with other business systems.

This and other factors result in low-level technical system requirements that typically can be only obtained from people in the development department that are familiar with the details of the operation of the existing systems.

Some latitude exists in what needs to be documented. If development is to be contracted out to a firm that is not familiar with the current system environment, many details must be documented. If the functional requirement will need to be tested as part of system testing, the requirement should be recorded. If the function would be obvious to the developer and will easily be understood when reading the actual code when performing maintenance one year after delivery, documentation is optional.

Functional Requirements Example

The example below represents the functional requirements that are an extension of the user requirements provided in Example 4 of Chapter 4.

1. The old key must exist in the investment table with an id equal to 3, which specifies that it is a foreign security ID.

2. The new key must exist in investment table with a code equal to 2, which indicates that it is a domestic securities number.

3. The new key must NOT exist in the investment table with a code of 4.

4. If the above conditions are true the update button will be enabled

5. If the update button is pressed, then :

   a) Update old SecKeyNum in Investment Purchase table with the new number for all investments where SourceCde is equal to 11, which represents the Source Exchange .

b) Update old SecKeyNum in SecID table with the new number for all investments where SecIDCde is equal to 7.

After the above processing, place two messages on the Recalculation Trigger queue for immediate processing.

The above operations must be performed as one transaction. This means if the first update is successful and the second update fails then the first update must roll back.

Database Considerations:

No new fields or tables are required.

There must be an audit trail of who made the modification.

Requirements Review

In the process of creating the functional requirements, the development team performs a review of the requirements. Their input is valuable in many ways. They could catch exploding tasks or missed tasks. They could suggest modifications that could speed development with little or no sacrifice in the ease of use. They can identify errors that were missed by the previous reviews and can recommend alternate controls to ease data entry. The business analyst should review any suggestion and if it results in a major change the users should be notified.

Database Design

All of the data fields that are documented in the user requirements must make their way to the database. New tables or extensions to existing tables must be defined using object or database design techniques.

Architecture

> *"Use Component-based Architectures . The process focuses on early development and base lining of a robust executable architecture, prior to committing resources for full-scale development. It describes how to design a resilient architecture that is flexible, accommodates change, is intuitively understandable, and promotes more effective software reuse. The Rational Unified Process supports component-based software development."* [Rational 2001]

Architecture is key to determining the tasks that need to be performed to complete the project. But what is Architecture? Here is a short list.

1. Choice of technology .Net or Java

2. Choice of database product, e.g. Oracle

3. Choice of code organization, e.g. two tier, multi-tier

4. Choice of middleware

5. Reference implementation of the model-view-controller functions and documentation

All of these should be chosen at the organization level and shared by all web projects. Savings can be obtained if all projects utilize the same tools and technologies and most of all, code organization. This may appear to be common sense, but it is surprising how many large companies cannot accomplish this.

If all the systems of an organization implement the model-view-controller functions in exactly the same way, maintenance, which is one of the largest costs, is minimized. A developer can easily be switched from one department to another and quickly become productive. The code organization is the same. The only difference is the data that is being processed. Later sections will go into this in detail.

There are additional benefits to standardization. The fewer technologies used in an IT organization, the better. This minimizes the number of skill sets that need to be maintained in the organization. I have been in very large organizations that have allowed various teams to choose the tools that they wanted. Anything could be justified based upon the ability to meet the scheduled dates. However, this created a maintenance nightmare.

Architecture cannot be static. It must be updated every few years. Technology moves forward, but constantly changing to use the latest technology serves to increase costs. Every time the organization architecture is changed both the old skill and the new skill needs to be available for many years in order to keep the software maintained. This causes increased costs, frustrations, and delays. All of these effects are difficult to explain and justify to the business side of the company.

In this book, Architecture means the generic components that are used to create a response to a web request. Each web request to a server causes some code to be executed. This code typically follows a pattern. For both Java and .Net technology best practice recommends separating the database access functions from the display functions. Best practice also recommends separating the logic that determines what should be displayed from the actual rendering of the HTML that goes back to the browser. Figure 5.1 illustrates this point.

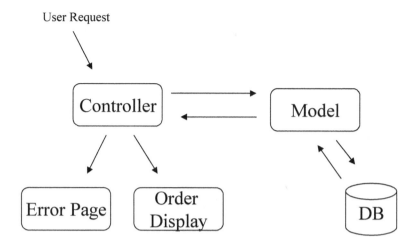

User Request

Controller

Model

Error Page

Order Display

DB

Figure 5.1. The classic MVC pattern for web development.

The pattern in Figure 5.1 is an instance of the Model View Controller design pattern for an web application:

> *Business Model* - all of the logic that is needed to manipulate the business data e.g. decrement inventory each time an order is created. Included in this logic are the functions of authorization and authentication.
>
> *View* - The logic that displays information to the user, i.e. creates the actual html that goes back to the browser.
>
> *Controller* - The logic that coordinates the interactions between the user actions, the model response and determines what View should be sent back to the browser.

Figure 6.1 can be used to explain how these three sections of a system work together to service a user's request. The controller receives the user request. The controller translates the request into terms that the Model understands and sends the request to the Model. The model authenticates the user and determines if they are authorized for the particular request. For example the model answers the following question. Is this a valid user id and login and can this person view salary history of an employee? If the request passes, the model retrieves the data and sends it back to the controller. The controller parses the response to determine what view to display to the user. For example if the Model determines that the user is not authorized for the request, the controller must display a different view than if the user was authorized. If the model determined if the user was authorized, but the request had no valid response (e.g. the order could not be found), the controller must display yet another view.

Estimating Pattern Part 1

An Internet site will have many independent instances of the MVC architecture. Each instance will service one or several http requests from a browser. **Determining the number of instances of the Model, View, and Controller components that need to be implemented is the key to identifying the number of tasks that are required to complete the project.**

Studies have shown that low level estimates are more accurate than those based upon little detail. Many organizations attempt to estimate at the use case level. What is proposed here are estimates based on the number of system components that will be required. This is at a much lower level than estimates made based upon use cases.

The Enterprise Architecture

Within each of these areas (View and Controller) for a given technological approach (Java or .Net) there is no consensus on how to architect a solution. In the Java world Struts is becoming accepted. In the .Net world, a Duwamish architecture, based upon a combined view/controller and a separated Model that contains a business façade, business rules, and data access layers. However, Microsoft is also recommending an architecture similar to Struts [Mortensen 2003] and Java Server Faces tends to duplicate the standard Microsoft architecture. There is still considerable variability in the interactions between the Model and the Control with regard to communications between the components and the location of the implementation of the model logic. For example the model logic could be implemented as a special set of classes, in a separate process (EJB or Web service), or as a stored procedure. In addition, for each of these different communications methods can be used such as web services or object remoting. Discussions of the details and tradeoffs will be left to other texts.

The chosen architecture must also account for items that are known to become sticky issues if left until the development phase of the project. These items include handling the back button, how to implement database transactions that span web requests and performance/hardware requirements.

The completed architecture should provide some estimate of the number of requests that can be served using a particular set of hardware. Technically there are many caveats in this type of estimate, but something is needed to identify potential hardware needs early in the project. These estimates can be refined during development but lead time for hardware purchases can be significant in an IT organization so it is best to have an early indicator of potential hardware requirements.

Another factor should be considered in the choice of architecture. There is a trade off between an elegant architecture and the required developer skill. If the chosen architecture uses many separate processes connected by uncommon communications methods, the learning curve for the development team can be significant and provide a hidden cost to all projects that need to use the architecture. In addition complex hard-to-learn architectures limit the availability of contractor supplementation of the development team. Each new contractor must be trained to use the new architecture.

The architecture should be chosen to provide the needed benefits with the minimum complexity. This provides the organization the ability to bring in contractors and new hires with the minimum learning curve. Simplicity also is related to reliability. If complexity means added code bulk, it could lead to higher defect rates and increase the cost of maintenance.

Architectures and frameworks should not be taken lightly by an organization. Their development is not a job for the novice programmer. The best, most knowledgeable architects and developers should be applied to this task. Alternatively, a company can utilize an architecture that has already been developed, tested and utilized by other organizations [Ceri, 2003].

Best practices dictate that the architecture should become a reusable component of the information architecture of an enterprise. Once the specific architecture is chosen, it must be fully tested. Each developer in the organization must become proficient at configuring the framework for the specific needs of the current project. It should be communicated to the development staff as a master implementation that can be used as a template. It must be well documented and perhaps be accompanied with a training program. Visual UML models of the architecture are critical for documenting and training purposes.

Implementation of the Architecture

Many instances of the MVC architecture are implemented in the construction phase of the project. For the project this means that the structure of the code that processes each URL has many similarities. Consequently, several things can be done to minimize the amount of original code that needs to be developed for the project. The standard method is the use of a framework that provides classes that implement the architecture and can be reused through inheritance and other programming constructs.

Master Template Pattern

> *"One key RUP principle that is less visible is to Automate what is human intensive, tedious, and error prone."*

Implementation of the architecture into a well-documented framework is important in minimizing the amount of new code that needs to be developed for a project. This can be taken one step further with the use of a master template approach. While the framework provides ways to access standard classes and methods, new code needs to be written to access them properly. This new code can have defects that would slow project progress. The template is the generic code that must be written to access the framework. The template is not completed code; it contains notes to the developer that marks where it must be customized to properly respond to a specific web request. A template could also have tags that can be replaced using string replacement programs e.g. Perl. This will replace the template tags with the proper naming conventions and creates a nearly complete implementation of the master template. This is repeated for each request/response in the system.

The major advantages of this methodology are:

1. The amount of new code developed for any system is minimized. This also decreases the amount of code that needs to be estimated in the planning process.

2. The architecture is always implemented in exactly the same way for each request response. This has large cost advantages with respect to maintenance. A developer unfamiliar with a system, but knowing the framework/template, can quickly pinpoint the location of a problem.

3. New projects become more predictable.

4. Success of a new system is less dependent upon the skill of the developer.

Clearly an organization has much to gain from adoption of the architecture framework/template approach.

With regard to the first item in the above list, Table 1 contains the number of lines of code needed to customize the templates for a page in a real project that used XML to communicate to the business model over MQ (IBM queue/messaging software).

Model		
–Create required SQL from request (20 - 50 Lines)		
–Business logic (0 – 200 Lines)		
–Convert DB response to XML (1 Line)		
Control		
–Send User ID to authorization bean (5)		
–Create required XML for model request (20-100)		
–Error handling (20-50)		
–Populate View Bean with model response (2)		
–Spawn proper jsp (1)		
JSP Page		
–Populate page with model response (25 - 150)		
–JavaScript data validation and control (25 - 150)		
Create View Bean (1)		

J2EE vs .NET

Much of the previous discussion is more applicable to the Java environment than to the .NET environment. The IDE of .NET provides a more constrained environment for creative architecture. The major remaining flexibility is in how session information is maintained, how the Model is implemented and how communication to the Model is implemented.

The enterprise template functionality incorporated into Visual Studio provides the template functionality that was previously discussed. Templates should be created for the model components consistent with the chosen architecture.

The template provided for a standard web application could be enhanced to provide more standard functions and become a template for the View/Control modules. User controls could also be used to automate and standardize other implementation of other architectural requirements. However, the logic of the estimating and planning techniques still hold. Visual Studio supports the master template approach through the use of the Enterprise Template.

For future discussions, the Control and View will be combined and be called Display. Consequently, the work will be planned based on tasks related to a Display component or a Model component.

Chapter 6 Work Planning & Estimating

Planning and Estimating Pattern

Another key task of the elaboration phase is the planning and estimation of the remainder of the project. The planning and estimating process will consist of three steps:

1. Identifying all of the tasks that need to be performed (work breakdown structure from previous section)

2. Estimating the duration of each task

3. Sequence the tasks

These tasks are best done sequentially.

Work Breakdown Structure

Where are we going now? One of the things that are required for any successful project is an accurate work breakdown structure. This is just basic project management as defined by PMBOK [PMI 2004]. It is logical that you have a list of the required tasks for a project before an estimate can be created. This list must include all tasks and be at a sufficiently low level to provide for easy estimation. In this domain it contains a list of the software components that need to be coded. The next sections will discuss a way to break down a project into its parts so that the programming tasks can be listed, i.e. create the work breakdown structure for the project. Basically the process follows these steps:

1. List the screen (display components)

2. List number of database accesses (model components)

3. Create a best case, worst case and most probable estimate for each component.

The WBS Pattern

The basic web model is that a browser sends a request and a server responds to that request. In a data-driven web application, the response executes an instance of the Control (MVC) that is designated to handle that request. Requests can be generated by a button click, a menu pick, or some other event on a page. Part of the specification process is determining what requests a system should respond to and what the response should be. This can be done using a transition diagram.

Theory and Practice

The following technique describes an idealistic method for the development of the work breakdown structure. It is illustrative of the theoretical technique. Once the theory of the methodology is understood the process can be abbreviated. Developing a comprehensive navigation diagram for the system is a very tedious, time-consuming task that can be eliminated.

Before discussing transition diagram first the MVC architecture needs to be considered. The display of the page will require the Control and View to be activated. For the following discussion the combination of Control and Views will be called Display. For each Display the Model may or may not need to be activated. For example, if the form's request data fails validation, there is no need to update the database.

A transition diagram (Figure 6.3) is simply a diagram that contains all of the pages that a system can display and arcs between the pages that show the possible transitions. A diagram of this type is valuable in determining all of the development tasks that are required.

The information to draw this diagram is obtained from the prototype. Note that a transition is not limited to those that go from one page to another. A page can have transitions that redisplay the page.

Figure 6.3 shows a simple transition diagram. The notation can be something simple like this figure, which is a variation of a UML state diagram. The goal is to capture the inter-page and intra-page transitions. Consequently, the diagram shows the pages of the system and the corresponding transitions. Each page transition represents a round trip from the browser to the server and an activation of an instance of the MVC. The request is made to the server and the server returns a page. Consequently, each transition causes some code on the server to execute. This method easily highlights the pages that are more difficult to code than others by identifying the number of unique transitions entering a page.

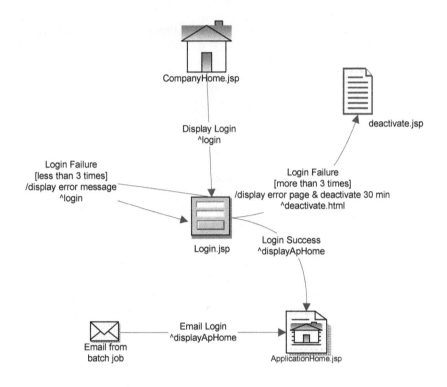

Figure 6.3 Simple Transition Diagram (see the section on shortcuts)

It is also interesting to note that no code will execute without a transition. Consequently, the project plan should contain a task for coding each transition. This fact is important to the planning process that will be discussed later. If the planning process is transition based, the forgotten task problem is nearly eliminated. Estimates will be made by asking how much code is needed to provide the functionality required by this transition.

Let's take a moment and look at the nomenclature of the transition. Each transition has a starting page and an ending page. The starting and ending page for a transition can be the same page. Each transition is labeled with up to 4 items Transition named "Login Failure B" has all four items listed.

- Login Failure B – Transition name (this is also the WBS task tracking name)

- [more than 3 times] – Guard condition – a condition that must be satisfied for the transition to be performed.

- /display error & deactivate 30 minutes – an action that is to be performed

- ^deactivate – the URI that the system will be redirected to when the user id should be deactivated

Note: this labeling task is sometimes eliminated. In many cases its cost is not justified by the value.

Value of Page Transition Diagrams

Part of the value of the transition diagram is that it forces the analyst to walk through the application. This thinking process will uncover items that are not defined well enough to provide instructions to the developer. Identifying these items at an early stage prevents delays during development caused by attempting to contact users to clarify the vague requirements.

In some cases the guard condition for the transition is more complex than what was shown in the previous example. In these cases the ultimate goal must be kept in mind. *Capture enough detail so that a developer can envision how much work will be needed to implement the page.* The basic reason for creating the diagrams is to identify the work that is needed so accurate estimates can be made. If the goal is kept in mind the development of the diagrams goes quite quickly. The following paragraphs describe some transitions with additional complexity.

The next figure (Figure 6.4) shows a transition from the home page of the application. This example is somewhat more complex because the display of the next page depends upon the user request and the response from the model. Remember the Control looks at the request, and also the response of the Model in order to determine what view to display.

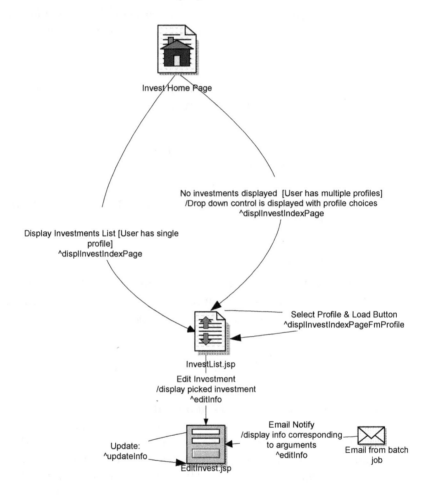

Figure 6.4 Additional guard conditions and email links (see the section on shortcuts)

Consider a bank application where a person can have multiple accounts. From the home page the user can display the detailed deposits and withdrawals for an account. If the person has only one account its details are displayed. Otherwise, the investments from one of the accounts are displayed and an additional control is displayed that will allow the user to chose another account. The Control has to query the Model and make a choice based upon the result.

Using the transition diagram this situation is shown with two parallel transitions, one for each condition. Alternatively, only one transition could be shown and the details captured in a note or a page use case. The goal is to minimize cost and clearly communicate the requirements to the developer. So use what serves the purpose best.

The transition can be even more complex. Besides the request and the response from the model, the state of the session or a variable in a cookie can affect the transition. This logic must be captured and communicated to the developer somehow.

Some transitions do not need to be placed on the transition diagram. Global transitions, such as a non-authenticated person attempting to access any page, should be handled as part of the architecture or master template and does not need to be estimated for each page. However, if there is work to be done to implement this functionality the developer needs to know about it so it will be included in the estimate.

Model Considerations

Now we must focus on the Model. For the purposes of this book the model portion of the architecture will consist of one round trip to the database, a SQL statement and a response set. Each transition may need to have one or more Model components activated to perform its work. For example, if a form has multiple dropdown menu controls, each must be filled by accessing their model. From the transition diagram it is easy to determine which transitions require a unique message from the model and which transitions require the same message. For example, in Figure 6.4, Email Notify and Login-Success will both require the same trip to the database to get the users investment information. A listing (Table 6.1) of the required transition, Display components (Jsp) and Model components can be derived from the diagram. From this listing the unique Model components can be determined. Each unique Model component will become a task in the work breakdown structure. The URI Reference is the control component.

Transition	URI Ref	Jsp	Model
Update	UpdateInfo	EditInvest.jsp	UpdateInvest
Email Notify	EditInfo	EditInvest.jsp	GetInvest
Edit Investment	EditInfo	EditInvest.jsp	GetInvest

Table 6.1 Part of a Module Listing from a Java web project.

Identifying Tasks Summary

The previous section discussed a technique that can be used to identify the tasks that are required for a project. These tasks form the basic work breakdown structure for the development portion of the project.

- Each URI reference maps to an instance of the Control template task.

- Each page maps to a jsp or aspx display task.

- The transition table will provide a list of the instances of the Model task that needs to be configured.

- In addition, there should be a task to create the basic HTML for the page.

- In addition to the above tasks other tasks such as creating batch jobs, environment setup, and testing tasks must also be included.

Once the tasks have been enumerated, the estimation process begins.

Reuse

Development of Table 6.1 should also take into account model components that have already been developed for other projects and are installed as services. Clearly, these should be reused for the new project.

Performance Considerations

If a reusable Model View Controller architecture is used as suggested previously, many questions about performance have been answered on previous projects. The risk of delivering a poorly performing system is minimized. While there are many instances that can be imagined to make this statement false, it is important to note that a new system is no more than creating instances of the MVC architecture. The code on a new system is not an unknown entity and should have performance similarities that could be used for predicting the performance of a new system.

Shortcuts

The goal of the above exercise was to develop a detailed work breakdown structure that can be easily estimated. After understanding the theory and getting some experience you will quickly learn to take short cuts to eliminate the tedious detail. Experienced architects and managers can provide the necessary work breakdown detail directly from the paper prototypes using common display patterns.

Common Display Patterns

The two key factors for estimates are the number of independent database queries (modal components) and the number of pages (display components). For example if a form has two dropdown menus, there would typically be five independent database queries to be implemented: one query to populate each of the two dropdowns and others to read, update and delete form data. These facts determine the number of data model components that will need to be implemented.

Window/page based interfaces have only a few major variations. Each of these requires one interaction with the model part of the MVC and can be used for quickly identifying the number and function of the needed model components.

1. The user enters search/filter criteria and then clicks a button to perform a search.

2. The system displays a list of records e.g. a list of bank transactions or customers within a zip code

3. From a list of records the user selects a record for editing. The unique key of the record is used in a query to find the record.

4. The user selects a record from a list and requests it to be deleted.

5. Display one record for editing

6. Edit/update a record

7. Create a record

8. Display a dropdown list. This will require a trip to the database to populate the dropdown.

There are two common patterns that utilize combinations of the items above.

- Maintain a many to many relationship. Figure 6.5 shows a common implementation of this.

- Maintain a many to one relationship. A master – detail form is an example of this.

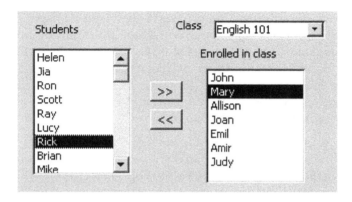

Figure 6.5 Many students attend many classes and each class has many students

Factoring requirements into a list of the required display and model tasks are the basis for estimation that is discussed in the following chapter.

Patterns for Estimating

Estimates for IT projects should be made by those who will do the work. Bottom up estimating provides the following benefits:

Better accuracy. *Estimates made by those who will do the work are more accurate because the person making the estimates has had experience executing similar work.*

Accountability. *Those who develop their own work estimates feel more accountable for their work. They also feel more accountable for success in meeting the estimates they have made.*

> Team empowerment. *Having team-developed dates as opposed to management-dictated dates empowers the team because the schedule is built on estimates that team members can accept as realistic. [Microsoft 2002b]*

Once all of the development tasks are identified they can be estimated. The person that will do the development, best performs estimates. In order for this to be an accurate estimate the information provided to the developer should completely describe the functionality that the developer needs to code. In reality this is much more difficult than it sounds. The ability of developers to estimate varies significantly.

What is about to be proposed is a variation of the Delphi [Kruchten 2002]. A team of developers and the project manager meet and discuss each page and the tasks required to implement the page. An estimate for each of the display and model components required to implement the page is then developed. The person who will be responsible for the implementation is the person who provides the estimate. However, all parties must be clear as to what the estimates means. **Is it the best-case scenario estimate or is it the worst case**?

Best Case, Worst Case, and Most Probable

In order to eliminate this potential misunderstanding, the developer provides **three estimates for each task: the best-case estimate, the worst case estimate and the most probable**. The project manager records these. By forcing the developer to focus on best/worst/most probable, more realistic estimates are obtained. Without this discussion, it is uncertain what an estimate from a developer really means. The process is conducted as a team to provide additional opinions and catch mistakes. Discussion should be encouraged about estimates that seem too low or too high.

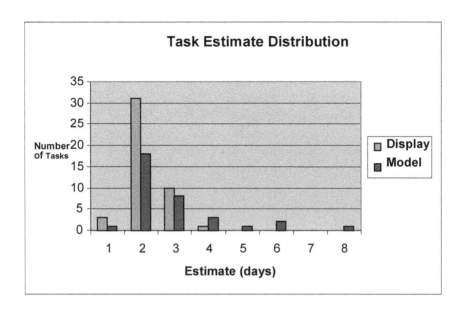

Figure 6.5 Distribution of the Display and Model tasks estimates.

Because the subject of this book is limited to data driven web sites that are built from templates as described in Chapter 5, estimates are more accurate. Model components are very similar to each other. Display components also have large amounts of similarity. This is not blue-sky, green-field development. It's based upon modifying Model and Display templates to fit the particular circumstance.

Quality assurance begins with the estimation process. There is no substitute for thorough unit testing. The developer should be informed that at least half of his time estimate should be for unit testing.

The result of this meeting is a list of estimates that are used to create the project plan. Figure 6.5 shows the distribution of the most probable task durations obtained for one delivery iteration.

If the organization architecture is stable for a long period of time a significant database of productivity for past projects can be developed. Past projects could then be used to estimate new projects. However, as Figure 6.5 suggests there can be large variations from page to page and simple scaling factors i.e. hours per page can provide misleading results. Consequently, the risk is much lower by performing the bottom up estimates of the work based upon the complete functional requirements.

Estimate Accuracy

Many times the financial system used for tracking actual cost does not provide fine granularity with regard tracking by task. Estimates are made at a lower level than can be tracked by the system. This is consistent with the standard project management principles for bottom-up estimating. Tracking is performed at a higher level than estimation [PMI, 2004]. Consequently, the work is grouped on a component basis. The tasks for the Views and Control component of a request are tracked as one display component. All of the related model services are tracked as a separate model component.

Figure 3.2 shows a comparison of the actual and estimated work for the model components of a project. Figure 8.2 shows a comparison of the actual and estimates for the display components of a project. On average, the techniques presented previously work with enough accuracy to predictably plan a project.

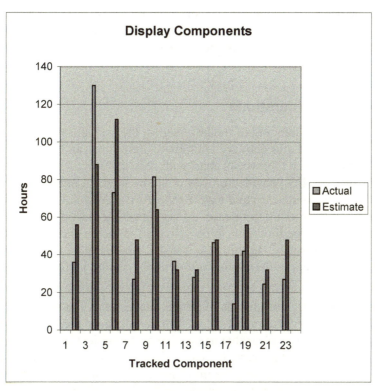

Figure 8.2 Comparison of the estimated and actual effort for the display components of a real project.

Incomplete Requirements

Requirements form the basis for the estimate. If requirements are incomplete, an estimate of this work must be obtained. The work can be bounded by postulating how much work is not documented in the requirements. For example an estimate can state as an assumption that it includes as contingency 10 additional instances of the MVC architecture accessing 10 tables. This statement provides flexibility in the resulting functionality and also a basis for project change control.

The last chapter of this book discusses the corporate planning cycle. Before final requirements are available some rough estimates are needed. Postulated requirements like the above can be used at any point in the corporate planning cycle to provide an estimate that has some basis. Later in the planning cycle estimates can be revised and convincing reasons can be given for changes in the estimates.

Delivery Iterations

Before sequencing of the task begins, the system should be partitioned into delivery iterations . Iterations can be relatively small only a few weeks apart with only a minor amount of functionality provided or they could be large taking several months to develop and test. Each iteration may not produce a useable production release. Many times interdependencies require several large functions to be delivered to the business simultaneously. In this case it is still beneficial to structure the project plan in iterations for to reduce risk and increase efficiency.

Figure 6.1 shows trends of project success as a function of project size. There are a multitude of factors that cause these trends. However, it is clear that as the size of the project increases, the probability of success decreases significantly. Consequently, structuring large projects into smaller self-contained projects (iterations) can reduce risk and are easier to manage than one large project.

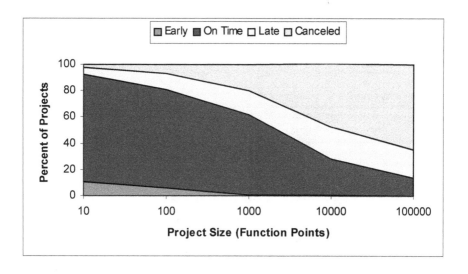

Figure 6.1 Project success probabilities versus project size [Jones 1998] (1000 function points is roughly 30 person weeks of work with good tools.)

> *The key to iterative development is to frequently produce working versions of the final system that have a subset of the required features. These working systems are short on functionality, but should otherwise be faithful to the demands of the final system. They should be fully integrated and as carefully tested as a final delivery [Fowler, 2005]*

Depending on the business process and the amount of functionality, iterations do not need to be released to the user community. In some cases several iterations will need to be completed before the system can be of any practical business value (Figure 6.2).

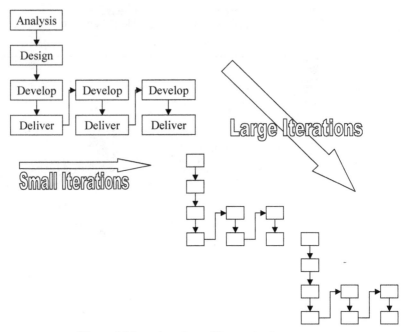

Figure 6.2 Iterations in an IT organization

Iterations can be chosen based upon many criteria. Here are some common factors that are used to segment and sequence the delivery:

Clear functionality categories – If the functions of the system are cleanly divided in more than one section, each section could be an iteration. For example, employees would be able to view the insurance benefits that they have signed up for when the first iteration is complete. After the second iteration they would be able to sign up for benefits using the Intranet.

Resource Constraints – For example, there is only one developer available for the next three months. The fist iteration is what is completed and tested at the end of that period.

User Availability – The users must be involved with the integration of the system into the business. This is done through user acceptance testing and training. The roll-out process can be costly. This may limit the number of production deliveries that can be made in a particular time period.

Risk Management – The high-risk portion of the system is delivered first. If the high-risk portion of the system fails, the remainder of the project can be halted.

Regression Testing Cost – Each production delivery should regression test the functionality that is currently operating in production. This overhead could be significant and limit the number of deliveries to a particular size or time frame.

Business Value – Some parts of the system may have more value than others. Requirements, which are clearly user gold platting, can be left to the last iteration. High value parts of the system could be delivered first. This also has the advantage that the stakeholders see the greatest value from the initial delivery (Glib, 1988). In most situations business value should be weighted the most heavily in determining iterations. The financial business benefits of a project are maximized when the benefits are provided as soon as possible. In addition, there are typically political advantages to providing what is most useful as soon as possible.

Support and Training – Once a system is released, the on going support and maintenance load will require significant resources. This cost will eventually need to be paid, but waiting until several iterations are complete may be used to delay this drain on development resources.

Task Sequencing

Once the tasks are estimated and placed in delivery iterations they may be sequenced. This is primarily driven by resource constraints and philosophy. One philosophy states that the model components should be developed first and completely unit tested before the display components are coded. This is useful if the model architecture is complex. Another more common philosophy is to develop a page and its required model components in adjacent tasks. Unrelated to philosophy is the constraint that the HTML web pages must be developed by a designer (and hopefully approved by the user) before the developer can breathe life into them with Java or .Net.

The Other Tasks

Once the actual development work is accurately estimated, the other project tasks can be estimated. These include tasks such as testing, rework (fixing defects) and project management. Testing should not be left to a two-week task at the end of the project. Testing should be done in parallel with development. When a developer is finished unit testing, it should undergo formal independent testing and any identified defects that are necessary to correct should be done quickly while the code is still fresh in the mind of the developer. Testing and defect corrections can be as much as 30% to 50% of the size of the development estimates.

Project management must also be added to the estimate. A rule of thumb is that managing one person takes approximately 10% of a person's time. One company that the author is familiar with desired each manager to have 12 to 15 people reporting to them. In very small projects with only a few developers, the manager is free to manage other projects or must play various roles such as tester, documentation specialist, dba, or some other tasks that complement the development team.

One item that is a common cause for project schedules to go awry is the overlooked task. This is some task found during development that was not accounted for on the original schedule. The techniques described in the previous sections can minimize this risk with regard to the functions that will be delivered. Other tasks like documentation must be independently identified. For tasks like these going over lists of commonly forgotten tasks can be helpful [McConnell 2006]. Among these is the setup of the development environment, developing documentation, user training, transition to production tasks, installation of demonstration sites and supporting these sites. This is list is only representative of the additional tasks that must be considered.

Contingency Planning

Contingency time should not be added by padding estimates for individual tasks. Since work expands to fill the time scheduled to do it (Parkinson's Law), the buffer will be absorbed by planned tasks, not unplanned events.

Contingency time should be scheduled as if it were another task. Typically, buffer is allocated immediately before major milestones, especially the later ones. It always should lie on the project's critical path. The critical path is the longest chain of dependent tasks in a project and directly determines the duration of the project.

As contingency time is expended over the course of the project, the remaining amount should be carefully tracked and conserved.

If a feature is added, or resources removed from the project, do not compensate by using contingency time. If you do, your ability to compensate for risk has been correspondingly reduced.

If all of the buffer time has been used, make the whole team aware that any disruption or delay is very likely to have a "knock on" effect and jeopardize the end date. [Mcrosoft 2002b]

How much contingency is enough to account for the unforeseen is part of every project? Using the previous techniques 10% of the most probable estimate has proven to be adequate. The use of the contingency budget should be used according to the guidelines documented by Microsoft.

Risk Management Plan

> *In the council's opinion, the absence of a comprehensive approach to risk management is a leading indicator of probable project failure. Effective risk management includes commitment of resources and the use of formal methods for identifying, monitoring, and managing risk. [Brown. 1996]*

Sometimes it is difficult to understand what can be done to manage risks. Aren't risks something out of our control? Risk management is the identification of risks and creating a plan to deal with the situation before the unplanned event happens.

The risk that needs to be planned are those that have a medium to high probability of occurring and if they occur will have a significant effect on the project. The risks that are not planned for are those that have a small effect regardless of probability (e.g. a ten minute network outage) or a significant effect with a very low probability (e.g. garbage truck hits the power transformer).

Some of the risks that need to be assessed in a web project are:

Loss of a key developer – With today's business environment people change positions frequently. A project should formally or informally have a backup plan. In addition, required scheduled check-in of intermediate work should be required.

Performance problems – Attack this risk as early as possible. The effect of finding a performance problem late in the project could be devastating. Sometimes a simple index may fix the problem. However, sometimes the fundamental architecture needs to be changed. Development project should take time early in the project to set up the proper environment. This is an environment that will provide an understanding of performance but may not be identical to the production system. Databases should be loaded to be significant percentage of the size of the production database.

Environment problems – Many times getting the proper development environment configured to work properly causes delays. One project that the author is familiar with required over two man-months and many calls to the vendor to install the development environment for a packaged system. Another common environment problem is caused by differences between the development, test, and production environments. When propagating code from the development environment, to the test environment and then to production environment differences are discovered that can cause significant delays.

Schedule risk – This is the most problematic for a project. The previous sections on project planning focus on reducing the risk in this area.

Chapter 7 Quality Management

Quality management is a very broad topic that would take volumes to cover in detail. It cannot be covered fully in this text. However a few ideas will be presented that can be used to reduce risk and cost.

According to standard project management methodology there is a project management knowledge area called Quality Management. It consists of three processes: Quality Planning, Quality Assurance, and Quality Control [PMBOK, 2004]. These processes are to be applied throughout a project not just at the end. Quality assurance and development begin at the same time. Quality must be built into the system by individual developers. Quality cannot wait until the end of development.

Problems with code quality at the end of a project can turn what looked like a successful project into a career-limiting event. There are a few things that can be done before construction begins and during construction to minimize the risk of poor quality.

Unit Testing

Unit testing is where the quality of the product is determined. Up to this point the business analyst has done their best to get agreement on what the code should do. The overall design has been embodied in a reusable architecture that has been tested and satisfies all environment, security and performance constraints. Now it's up to the developer to do their job. A key quality assurance task is instituting a process to verify that the developer performs sufficient tests to certify what they turn over is near perfect.

The project manager can sit back and trust that all the developers test their code perfectly or institute quality assurance. A repeatable process that provides a high level of quality, regardless of the developer capability, requires action. This takes the form of code reviews and unit test reviews. Code reviews are well documented. A discussion of unit test reviews follows.

What basically must be assured is that the developer has thought of and performed a sufficient set of tests. The key words here are "thought of." Testing to some extent is a creative process. Most developers can come up with a set of test that covers a significant amount of the functionality. Increasing this percentage closer to 100% for all developers all the time is the quality assurance task.

Two principles can be used to aid this task:

- One plus one is greater than two

- If a manager focuses on something, developers will pay more attention to it.

Let's consider the first item. When two people work together on a creative process, they typically enhance each other's capability and the result is better than either of them could do alone. The methodology of Extreme Programming uses this technique. What I propose is Extreme Testing. This can take several different forms. The developer creates a spreadsheet of the tests that he has performed and reviews this with another developer or a group of developers. In past projects I have had testers sit down with developers to develop test plans. This isn't really a review. It is a collaboration to verify near-complete testing. It's two people working together with the goal of perfection.

The use of unit testing tools like junit or nunit are best practices, but can add significantly to the amount of code that needs to be developed and will consequently increases cost. Using these tools comprehensively may not be consistent with the goal of reducing project ceremony and cost. The tools should be used pragmatically not dogmatically by identifying parts of the system that would benefit.

Let's now consider the second bullet item. This is a basic principle of psychology termed the Hawthorne effect. This refers to improvements in productivity or quality, which results because the workers are aware of extra attention being paid to them [http://en.wikipedia.org/wiki/Hawthorne_ studies]. Test coverage should improve simply because there is a quality assurance task expected for each package that leaves a developers desk. If a review of a test plan does not identify any additional test, it doesn't mean that the review was useless. According to the principle, more focus has been placed on quality, which results in better quality.

Final Developer Testing

Professional testers will take the requirements for a project and convert them to a test plan. These test plans should be provided to the developers so that they can perform the tests (to the extent that they are able) before turning over the code for final testing. Two sets of test data should be created. Both cover the same scenarios but use different data. One set will be used by development to verify the operation of the system. The testers will use the other set in the final testing of the system. This type of open-book testing minimizes the amount of rework and retesting that occurs. It also focuses the developer on critical tasks that the system needs to perform.

System Testing

> *"The purpose of independent testing is to provide a different perspective and, therefore, different tests; furthermore to conduct those tests in a richer [...] environment than is possible for the developer." [Beizer 1995]*

While testers provide testing independent of the developer, they are part of the development team and need to have the team goal in mind. Their relationship and communication with the developers should be excellent. Their attitude should be they are helping the developers perfect their code. They should not have the attitude of a supreme being in control of the project.

Test plans

Detailed test plans should be created early in the project after the requirements are complete. The process of creating the plans could identify errors in the requirements documents. This is part of the refinement iteration that is done early when correction of the mistakes is inexpensive.

Graph-Based Testing

Coverage and documentation of the tests to be performed can be time consuming and expensive. One interesting method [Richardson 2003] uses graphs of the system that are similar to the page transition diagrams described in Chapter 6. These are used to determine the paths through the system to be tested. Most of the cost of developing word-based test scripts is eliminated instead a copy of the transition diagrams is used for each test. The path through the system for the test is identified. Only the data to be entered on each page during the test needs to be documented. The format of the requirements document facilitates this task. Different test cases can reuse the same path with a different data set to stress boundaries of the system. If the graph is comprehensive and up-to-date, full coverage with regard to paths through the system can be developed.

Testing Environment

Functional testing must be performed using all of the browsers that are part of the system requirements. In addition, if the number of end users or if the transaction rate is expected to be high, load testing must also be performed. This will require special environments and tools.

Intranet systems are far less expensive to test than Internet systems. Internal systems are typically limited to a single browser and a few operating systems. External systems must be tested with far more browsers and operating systems.

Testing with a variety of browsers, their older versions and different operating systems requires planning. Lead times to procure and install the testing environment could be a significant task.

One of the biggest risks of a system is performance. This is particularly true for service-oriented architectures where multiple processes communicate in order to service a web request. What works in development will not necessarily perform well in production. The development database should be of significant size to identify performance problems during development. This is done to identify performance bottlenecks early in the cycle.

Test Sequencing

Earlier in the text the development of the testing scenarios was discussed. The sequence of the tests should be considered. Testing the major functions of the system should occur first followed by other tests in the order of importance to the overall functionality of the system.

Test Progress Tracking

One of the key issues with testing is determining and reporting the status of the task. There are various metrics that can be used to indicate nearness of completion.

- Number of tests executed
- Number of tests passed
- Number of tests failed

The test scenarios provide a convenient method of tracking the testing progress. If 30 scenarios have been planned, testing is approximately 50% done when 15 have been completed.

User Acceptance Testing

After development and system testing is complete, an important step in the delivery of a system is user acceptance testing (UAT). In this process actual users sit down with the system and perform the tasks that they are expected to perform on the production system. This process is key in reducing delivery risks. One would assume that after going through system integration testing the users would not find any problems that would prevent them performing their work. However, this is not proven by the author's experience. Many times very serious flaws make it through system testing. UAT minimizes risk of delivering a system that cannot be used in production and needs to be backed-out. This is a particularly severe and embarrassing problem.

User Acceptance Testing requires a significant amount of planning. It should not be a haphazard, poke-at-it task. It should be well organized and scenario based. In other words, scripts should be developed that cover the day-to-day tasks of the user. The scripts should contain the exact data to be used in the script. For example if the system was going to add an insurance policy, the name, address and other needed information should be contained in the script. This allows the scripts to be reproducible.

Several data sets may be required. Each test case should cover a special anomaly that could cause the system a problem. For example, adding an insurance policy for someone in a zip code that spans a state border. Many times users are very familiar with the anomalies that cause problems. Users are required to execute these scripts to ensure proper coverage of all of their key tasks.

If possible variations of these data sets should be given to the developers early in the process for open book testing. Also testers should perform these test prior to UAT. If this is done UAT should only be a formality.

The number of scenarios that were stopped in UAT because of an insurmountable defect that prevented accomplishing a business task is an indicator of the production readiness of the system. In some cases if UAT identifies many shortcomings that require significant rework, UAT may need to be repeated after corrections are made.

Also note that there are various degrees of passing a test and various types of defects (as shown below). Systems can go into production with defects if the business tasks can still be performed. There are very few perfect systems currently in production anywhere in the world.

- Critical: The business process cannot be performed without this modification.

- Important Defect: System is still useable, by using an awkward work-around or a non-critical error exists.

- Important Enhancement: Will add significantly to the value provided by the system.

- Enhancement: Will provide some added value to the system

- Defect: All other defects

Chapter 8 Construction

Communications Pattern

One of the principles recommended by MSF [Microsoft, 2002a] and RUP [Kroll 2005] is open communications. This is particularly true during construction. The construction period may take months. During this period a dialog should be continued with the stakeholders. This serves various purposes. First, stakeholders are very busy people with many things on their minds. Over a period of months they can forget key decisions that they have made concerning requirements. When the final development is presented for user acceptance, the stakeholder may forget the rational behind their decision and change the requirements. Review of preliminary results will keep the decisions and the project fresh in mind. For example, the first iteration delivery will provide only a subset of the functionality of the final system. The stakeholders may forget the decision about the functionality in the first delivery and expect a much broader set of functionality. A disappointed or disgruntled stakeholder may result. Keeping the project fresh in the mind of the stakeholders by holding frequent reviews is in the best interest of the project.

One of the most important tasks during the construction phase is to communicate with the future users of the system. During construction keep all levels of users involved. Meet with users and demonstrate what is being accomplished. Remind them of the requirements that were agreed upon.

A print of each final HTML page should be provided to the SMEs. Obtain their review and approval of the final pages as soon as the pages can be visually demonstrated. Meet with the SMEs regularly to review the construction progress. They will appreciate shorter meetings. Do not feel obligated to schedule a full hour if there are only a few items to discuss. They are very busy people and will appreciate being informed in the minimum time required.

Meet with upper management in the user community to make sure they are receiving the correct information. Do not depend on your upper management to effectively communicate your project to the upper management of the user community. Typically your management has many more issues to be discussed and your project many have low priority especially if the project is going well. Keep from being a development black hole where the requirements from the users go in but no information about progress goes out.

Schedule frequent regular internal team meetings to discuss progress and problems. Three times per week spaced with approximately the same amount working time between works well. For example, Monday morning, Tuesday afternoon, and Thursday afternoon allows approximately the same amount of time between meetings. As with previous meetings, these do not need to be long meetings. Keep the pace of the meeting fast moving so people do not get bored, table side discussions, and finish as quickly as possible.

Task List Pattern

> *"An effective team, members are empowered to deliver their own commitments." [Microsof, 2002b]*

There is a principle of psychology called Parkinson's Law the states that a task will expand to fill the allotted time. This is a very real force that needs to be managed. Developers need to be trained to take the task deadlines seriously. Another principle of good development practice is to allow developers flexibility in meeting schedules. They should be allowed to work ahead on the next task before the current scheduled task is completed. A developer should be given a to-do list with due dates of the tasks that they need to accomplish and be allowed to work a few tasks ahead if working ahead helps them work more efficiently. They are responsible for managing their own to-do list. They are allowed to be a day or two late on a task if they have worked ahead and show at least that much progress on future tasks. In this way both principles are satisfied.

Another technique to be taken into consideration is the Pygmalion effect. The Pygmalion effect (or Rosenthal effect) refers to situations in which students performed better than other students, simply because they were expected to do so [http://en.wikipedia.org/wiki/Pygmalion_effect]. Having an up-beat attitude and expecting the best can have good results.

Progress Tracking Patterns

> *The fifth practice is concerned with making sure that project planning and monitoring are based on a sufficient level of detail. "Inch pebble" refers to the need for detailed work plans at the level where each task is of a single type, is sufficiently small, and is assigned to a single point of responsibility. "Binary quality gates" refers to the use of objective acceptance criteria such that each output is either acceptable and complete, or is not acceptable and therefore not complete. Brown. 1996*

Using earned value techniques to determine if a project is doing well or poorly requires the measurement of three variables at a consistent point in the project. The first is the earned value (EV) of the work performed. The second is the planned value (PV) of the work that was expected to have been completed using the project plan. The last is the actual cost (AC) which is the amount of money actual spent. There can be issues with obtaining the needed measurements.

Earned Value

In order to determine the earned value, the estimate of completion for each task in the project must be obtained. This requires developers to estimate the amount of completion for the tasks that they are working on. Most seasoned project managers have had the privilege of managing the developer who is always 90% done. This is typically caused by the developer assuming that the task is complete as soon as the code has been written without giving enough thought to the testing process. Establishing the 50/40/10-tracking rule helps eliminate this type of problem.

The **50/40/10 rule** was originally mentioned in the previous section on estimation. The time duration for each development task is assumed to be distributed to 50 % coding, 40% testing and 10% to documentation/review. When a developer reports their progress, they must report the percentage done of each. Consistent with the binary gates principle, tracking credit is not given until each are reported as complete.

Actual Cost

Unfortunately most organizations do not use a single system to track developer time spent on a project and the actual amount of progress that is made. Cost tracking is typically a system established to collect the project costs for financial accounting reasons and to track vacations. This system typically operates independently of the project planning system that is used to provide the other two measures. Differences between the date that data is available from the finance system and the planning system date can cause difficulties with proper progress reporting.

Planned Value

Planned value is the easiest to obtain. It comes directly from the project baseline. The project-planning tool that you are using should provide this.

Reporting Progress

Tracking progress has several purposes. It provides the team a way of judging their progress. It also provides a way for management to evaluate the progress. In order to accomplish these goals the progress should be presented in an easily understandable manner. Earned value techniques are generally regarded as the best method of tracking progress [PMI 2004]. Comparing earned value (i.e., budgeted costs) with the actual costs of the work performed provides a fundamental indicator of cost/schedule performance problems.

However, the earned value measurements such as Cost Variance and Schedule variance can be somewhat confusing. Is a positive variance good or bad? In addition, the accuracy of the variance is dependent on getting all of the cost and performance measurements on the same date. Last, sometimes there is sensitivity in broadcasting to a large audience how much a project is actually costing.

Figure 8.1 from an actual project, shows one method that can be used to minimize the issues with regard to reporting progress.

There are three lines on this plot. One represents the percent complete based upon the project plan (labor only using a blended rate). It basically shows the expected progress of the project based upon the original project planning. Another line represents the percent complete of the project. This is obtained totaling the amount of planned work in the completed tasks and dividing that by the total work scheduled for the project. The last line is the percent spent. This is based upon the current project expenditures divided by the projected project costs.

In a perfectly planned project all three lines would coincide. Even better the percent complete would track above the plan and the percent spent would track below the plan.

A graph of this type published weekly during a project, provides more information about a project progress than a simple variance. The trends provide a history of where the project has been. In addition, they can be projected into the future more accurately. If the slope of the actual costs is much greater than the slope or the earned value line, a significant problem would be clearly evident. The standard earned value method would show a small problem with the project when the line crossed. The estimate of the cost overrun would then increase weekly by the amount of the difference between the two lines.

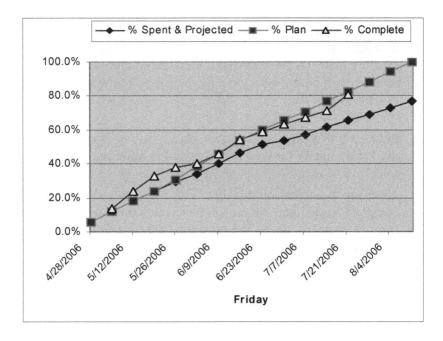

Figure 8.1 Progress tracking chart -- The team has completed 80% of the work and is expected to be over 20% under plan at the end of the project.

Sharing information like that shown in Figure 8.1 to the project team weekly helps motivate the team. If they are truly team members they will attempt to beat their schedules to aid others that are lagging. Without this information, a team member is only an individual trying to meet their personal schedules.

Other Methods of Progress Reporting

If a team is motivated to performing they enjoy the ability of seeing how they are doing. The project may provide other measures of progress that may be more meaningful to the team. If the project requires a large number of reports to be converted, the progress charts could be plotted with the number of reports converted versus the plan. Any appropriate measure can be used to provide feedback to the team.

Team Morale Pattern

Team building and having fun at work is an important task for the project manager. This process is highly personality dependent. This is not only the personality of the individuals on the team, but also the personalities of the project manager. The tone and culture of the organization also plays a part.

The development process that is described in this book can become tedious. A developer that has been chosen to be the expert in developing model components will become very good at it in a short time. Consequently, the job can become tedious. Job rotation can help. A model component expert can be rotated to be a display developer. Alternatively, a developer can be responsible for all the components for a group of web requests. Other than providing this variety, there is little that a project manager has direct control of.

Another possibility is to use the technique used by Pike Place Fish Market in Seattle [http://www.pikeplacefish.com/funstuff/sightsnsounds.htm]. Selling fish in a market can be a very tedious task. However, this market has become a renowned example of how to rise above the boring task and have fun at work. Things can be done to provide this vision and foster this attitude. "Fun at Work" committees can be established to identify activities and work on attitudes.

Establish Standards and Guidelines

The architecture should also be reviewed with the team if they are unfamiliar with it. They must understand where the templates need to be configured to support their coding tasks.

Along with reviewing the patterns, naming standards and commenting standards should be reviewed. One naming standard that the author has found useful is to use the name of elements in the database throughout the code. This means that if the element is passed in an XML message it retains the same name. Similarly if the element appears on a web page, the tag value should be the element name. Consequently, from the UI to the database the common element names are preserved. While this may not be a project time saver, it aids subsequent maintenance tasks significantly. With today's multilayered architectures, changing names in one of the layers makes problem diagnosis more obscure.

Project Development Hygiene

There are two fundamental processes in software development, which vary significantly from project to project. This is configuration management and promotion to production. Configuration management refers to the ability to restore software to a previous state. Many products are available to perform this task. They are not expensive or time consuming to use and can significantly reduce risk. There is no reason not to use a tool like this.

Regular offsite backup of interim software falls into the same category. For little cost a significant risk is eliminated.

Configuration management is another area that can cause some embarrassing problems when defects that were previously fixed appear again in production. A clear, well-defined check-in and promotion process cost little and reduces risk, headaches and keeps good relations with users.

Another aspect of development hygiene is *cleaning up the garbage*. Many times in web development, project's new images and other files become obsolete, but are not removed from the test or production environment because no one is sure if they are still being used. Sometimes this problem can get so bad that it is nearly impossible to determine what is actually being utilized by the production system. The promotion process should also consider elements that are no longer used and need to be removed from the test and production environments.

Scope Creep Anti-Pattern

Scope management is one of the key jobs of a project manager. Developer gold plating is the act of adding additional functionality to the system that is not in the requirements. Many of these changes are initiated internally in the team and must be controlled. The argument comes down to "I can make this better" versus "It's good enough." Forces from the user community will also attempt to add functionality to the system that was not originally agreed to. This is the typical scope- creep process. Changes must be fully documented and the funding identified, otherwise they must be left for another project in the future to implement.

Chapter 9 Transition to Production

Of all the phases, transition is the most diverse. The tasks that are needed can vary widely depending upon many factors. For example, the amount of user training that needs to be provided depends upon the complexity of the user interface and if the system is Intranet or Internet application. The entire introduction process will depend upon similar factors. Moreover, the culture of the IS organization, will dictate tasks that must be performed in order to handoff the system to operations and maintenance staff.

Preparing for Production

This phase includes many tasks that are not under the direct control of the project manager. The computer operations department must set up servers, firewalls and networks. Mechanism must be put in place to provide user passwords with the proper permissions. Databases will need to be created and populated. There are no short cuts in this task. The number and type of functions that need to be performed here vary widely from project to project and cannot be adequately treated by a general template approach. In a large industrial environment, a mature release process provides a means of making sure that nothing is missed.

User Documentation the Easy Way

For internal systems, there is usually an expectation of providing some user documentation. Sometimes requirements documentation can be morphed to provide this document by replacing the prototype screens with screen prints of the actual system. This document provides detailed explanations of the processes that occur when any button is clicked.

The problem is that the requirements documentation must be kept up-to-date. In the heat of the development some conscious decisions could be made based upon unforeseen circumstances that cause redirections of the architecture or the prototype screens. During development, personnel will roll on and off of the project. Knowledge may be lost in this process. Consequently, it is important to go back and update the documentation as the project progresses so that there is little to be corrected at the end and the documentation could be turned over to the testers, users and maintenance staff.

User Training

For Intranet systems, user training is not given enough emphasis. I have witnessed IS departments dump a system on a person's desktop with little or no additional information. The project manager is responsible for planning the system introduction process. For a rollout to a large dispersed organization, this could be quite time consuming and expensive. Overview meetings to inform the end user community, training material and training delivery (whatever form it takes) must be factored into the project plan.

Handoff to Maintenance

In some organizations, the maintenance programmers are different from the development team. Consequently, delivery of the system will require the review and approval of the maintenance personnel. In order to prevent last minute surprises, soliciting what are to be expected in advance of the handoff is desirable.

Project Closure

One of the last tasks of the project manager is to obtain approval from the stakeholders of completion. This is the final project sign-off and provides an agreed ending point. Discussions with the stakeholders preparing them for the final sign-off are necessary. Agreement upon what constitutes completion must be obtained well before the request for sign-off. The stakeholder may not fully understand what has been delivered or to what extent it has been tested. Providing this information in advance of the signing will provide a comfort level sufficient to obtain final approval.

Extension to Other Types of Projects

The preceding chapters discussed patterns that can be used to develop web-based data driven systems. The frequency of this type of project in a typical IT organization is relatively high. Because of this high frequency, the patterns can be easily understood and adjusted according to the environment and personality of the organization.

There are other mayor categories of projects such as: data warehouse, desktop upgrades, data center movement and infrastructure improvement. There are many others. Each of these has patterns, but in many cases the frequency of the project types are so low, the patterns are not easily recognized. With a low experience base it is almost impossible to create a comprehensive work breakdown structure. Critical tasks can be easily missed which result in large underestimates of the project cost.

Since experience in these projects is not available in-house, there are two alternatives. First, look for books that cover the topic. For example in the case of data warehouse projects, Chapter 3 of Kimball's (Kimball, 1998) is a classic resource. It has templates for a typical project plan. Some things can also be taken from this book. In this case iterative requirements capture discussed in the previous chapters is appropriate. Iterative development and deployment is also encouraged. The author was once part of a successful 4-year project that developed an investment data warehouse. It had several phases that delivered parts of the system.

The second alternative for developing and planning a project in an unfamiliar domain is to contact an expert, someone who has worked for several companies performing these tasks. Experience and a good clear-thinking mind can be a significant help in planning and identifying risks.

Chapter 10 PMO

The Role of the PMO

The Project Management Office (PMO) is becoming common in today's large IT organizations. The PMO is a department that has responsibility for projects. They can provide value to the project management process and can be a significant aid in meeting the project goals. This organization is not a group of lawyers policing adherence to penumbra of the standard processes. Nor are they a central planning authority, or a Gestapo. The PMO and the project manager work together, pushing on the same side of the project rock, trying to get it up the triple constraint hill. The PMO should be a kind, gentle spirit helping people to do their work.

To do this the PMO has various roles:

- Enterprise Investment Planning -- Ensuring a consistent presentation of proposed projects to upper management. This includes establishing standard methods of creating early estimates and consistent methods of estimating benefits.

- Resource Management -- Providing a framework where resources can be equitably distributed among projects.

- Tracking -- Provide consistent methods of tracking and reporting project progress.

- Guidelines -- Establishing project management standards and training in their use.

- Process Auditing -- Ensuring project management standards are being used consistently and software is developed at the minimum cost.

- Risk management and contingency budget management – Project managers must submit requests to use contingency budgets.

- Political Support -- Resources to help break log jams where project progress is being hindered by politics and personalities.

- Contingency management – A project manager must apply to use the contingency allocated to the project.

Corporate Planning Process

Earlier in the book the corporate planning process was mentioned. This is a key process that aligns the goals of the business with the investment in projects. High return on investment depends upon a reasonable planning process and good project management. Unfortunately, this process tends to attract special personalities and large committees, which result in impediment and delay. The ultimate process moves swiftly and sets a fast pace for coming to accurate decisions that provide high return on investment.

There are many alternative ways to organize a PMO with respect to an IT department. Many companies have a token PMO that provides some guidelines and logistical support. However, the most efficient process puts more control in the hands of the PMO. If all business analysts (BA) and project managers (PM) report to the PMO the project planning process can proceed without delays, and projects can be efficiently managed.

There are advantages to have all PM's working as a team to manage the projects within an IT organization. They can be shared among projects and they can back each other up.

Moreover, having the PM's in the PMO, encourages consistency of process among projects.

Process Strawman

Here is a strawman for an efficient corporate planning process. Note that this is a continuous process not a once-per-year event.

1. Any manager in the IS or Business can submit an idea for a project by sending an email to the PMO.

2. Within one week, a business analyst identifies the stakeholders and schedule interviews.

3. Within a short period the project charter is submitted to the PMO. The charter contains an evaluation of the potential benefits and cost. Since the evaluation is done by one of a team of BA's that reports to the PMO there is some basis to believe that the evaluation is fair and consistent with other evaluations.

4. The PMO makes a quick decision as to the value and places it on the project totem pole (ranking of all the outstanding projects).

5. As funding is made available by the corporate investment planning process, the PMO presents the best alternatives for management consideration. Projects move into the next phase where full requirements are developed and the project is reevaluated. If the financial evaluation has not changed, the project proceeds to the design and development phase. If the financial evaluation has changed the project is tabled or is placed back on the totem pole. Clearly not all projects will make it through this stage.

The above process must be carefully planned to execute with a **minimum of red tape** and allow it to proceed at a high rate of speed. The people responsible for analysis of projects need to be seasoned mature individuals. The people are the most important aspect of a PMO. Seasoned, clear thinking communicators that understand project management and the business are required. People that are good managers but are not known for thinking outside the box need not apply.

References

Beizer 1995   Beizer, Boris. Black Box Testing. New York, NY:
                 John Wiley & Sons, Inc. 1995

Beck 2001   Beck, Kent, Martin Fowler, Planning Extreme
                 Programming, Addison Wesley, 2001

Boehm 1995   Boehm, B, Clark, E. Horowitz, C Westland, R.,
                 Cost, Models for Future Life Cycle Processes:
                 COCOMO 2.0, Annals of Software Engineering,
                 Springer 1995

Brown. 1996   Brown, Norm. 1996. "Industrial-Strength
                 Management Strategies," IEEE Software, July
                 1996

Ceri, 2003   CERI, P Fraternali, A. Bongio, M. Brambilla, S.
                 Comai, M. Matera, Designing Data-Intensive Web
                 Applications, S., Morgan Kaufmann Publishers,
                 2003

Fowler 2005   Fowler, Martin, The New Methodology,
                 http://www.martinfowler.com/articles/newMethod
                 o logy.html#id2249833

Glib 1988   Glib, Tom, Principles of Software Engineering
                 Management, Addison Wesley, 1988

Grand, 1999   Grand, Mark Patterns in Java Volume 2, John
                   Wiley & Sons Inc., 1999

Humphrey   Humphrey, Watts, Managing the Software
1990   Process, SEI Series In Software Engineering,
                   Addison Wesley, 1990

Kimbal, 1998   Kimbal, Ralph, Larua Reeves, Margy Ross,
                   Warren Thornthwaite, The Data Warehouse
                   Lifecycle Toolkit, Wiley, 1998

Kroll 2003   Kroll, Per and Philippe Kruchten, The Rational
                   Unified Process Made Easy – A Practitioner's
                   Guide to the RUP, Addison Wesley, 2003.

Kroll 2005   Krol, Per, Walker, Royce, Key principles for
                   business-driven development, IBM
                   developerWorks, IBM, 2005

Kruchten   Kruchten, Philippe, Planning an Iterative Project,
2002   The Rational Edge, Rational Software 2002
                   http://www-
                   128.ibm.com/developerworks/rational/library/conte
                   nt/RationalEdge/oct02/IterativePlanning_TheRatio
                   nalEdge_Oct02.pdf

Kruchten   Kruchten, Philippe, Agility with the RUP, The
2002   Rational Edge, Rational Software 2002

Larman 2004   Larman, Craig, , Agile & Iterative Development,
                   Addison Wesley, 2004

McConnel   McConnel, Steve, Rapid Development, Microsoft
1996   Press 1996

Microsoft   MSF Team, Microsoft Solutions Framework
2002a   Version 3 - MFS Process Model V 3.1, White
                   Papers, Microsoft 2002,
                   http://www.microsoft.com/downloads/details.aspx?
                   FamilyID=e481cb0b-ac05-42a6-bab8-

fc886956790e&DisplayLang=en

Microsoft 2002b — MSF Team, Microsoft Solutions Framework – MSF Project Management Discipline V. 1.1, Microsoft 2002

Mortensen, 2003 — Mortensen, M.K., R. Mcgovern, C. Liptaak, ASP.NET and Struts: Web Application Architectures http://msdn.microsoft.com/library/en-us/dnaspp/html/ASPNet-ASPNet-J2EE-Struts.asp

PMI, 2004 — PMI, Guide to the Project Management Body of Knowledge, Project Management Institute, Newton Square, PA 2004

Probasco 2000 — Probasco, Leslee. The Ten Essentials of RUP—the Essence of an Effective Development Process, Rational Software White Paper, TP177, 9/00

Rational 2001 — Rational Unified Process Best Practices for Software Development Teams Rational Software White Paper TP026B, Rev 11/01 www.augustana.ab.ca/~mohrj/courses/2000.winter /csc220/papers/rup_best_practices/rup_bestpractic es.pdf

Richardson 2003 — Richardson, Alan. Practical Experiences in Graph-Based Testing, Presentation at StarEast 2003, www.compendiumdev.co.uk/stareast2003/stareast 2003.php

Standish 1994 — The Standish Group International, The CHAOS Report, , Inc.,1994, http://www.standishgroup.com/sample_research /chaos_1994_1.php

www.ingramcontent.com/pod-product-compliance
Lightning Source LLC
Chambersburg PA
CBHW051251050326
40689CB00007B/1149